# I PLAYED FOR COACH OSBORNE

# I PLAYED FOR COACH OSBORNE

## BOB SCHALLER

## I PLAYED FOR COACH OSBORNE

Bob Schaller, I Played for Coach Osborne

ISBN 0-9648992-4-8

Nebraska Book Publishing Company
A Division of Nebraska Book Company, Inc.
4700 South 19th
P.O. Box 80529
Lincoln, NE 68512
(402) 421-7300

Library of Congress Cataloging in Publication Data in Progress.

Distributed by:

Cross Training Publishing
317 West Second Street
Grand Island, NE 68801
1-800-430-8588

Photo Credit: All photos Copyright © 1998 by Gordon Thiessen, and UNL Photography: Richard Wright, Richard Voges and Tom Slocum.
Cover Design: Gordon Thiessen / Cross Training Publishing
Cover photo by Gordon Thiessen / background photo by UNL Photography.

nebraska book
publishing

To my 4-year-old son Garrett, who, while I wrote this book, kept giving me three choices when I had to leave for a while to finish it: "Daddy, stay home, stay home or stay home."

Well Garrett, now that we have the time, we will put on our "Husker National Champion" sweatshirts and spend some time at home, watching the 1995 Orange Bowl, 1996 Fiesta Bowl and 1998 Orange Bowl.

# A C K N O W L E D G M E N T S

Thanks to Gene Cotter, a University of Nebraska alum who did the interviews with the players from Coach Osborne's final team for this book. A special thanks to Gordon Thiessen of Cross Training Publishing and Tom Swanson of Nebraska Book Publishing for making this idea a reality. There will likely be scores of books to follow on Coach Tom Osborne's legacy, but it is hard to imagine one written by, and for, those who truly care about the University of Nebraska, the coaches and players, and what the entire state truly stands for.

# TABLE OF CONTENTS

Tom Osborne's legacy at Nebraska is about more than winning football games. In fact, it is about a way of life that is not measured on a scoreboard or by team records.

Certainly the success the program has had under Coach Osborne is impressive. The national championships and 255 victories are a good measuring stick for on-the-field success. But the University of Nebraska football program is also about a different kind of success. What Coach Osborne and the staff have striven for each year is to help each player in the program grow. We want the players to reach their potential academically, personally and athletically. This kind of growth has been a key factor in our success both on and off the field during Coach Osborne's 25 years.

I am honored to follow in Coach Osborne's footsteps. To ensure that we continue heading down the right path, I will apply what I have learned in my 19 years under Coach Osborne.

As you will read in this book, Coach Osborne, and the rest of the coaching staff, have always been concerned about far more than records. We have always tried to affect the most positive influence on our players. One of the many things that Coach Osborne was so good at was recognizing that players are different. They come from different backgrounds: socially, athletically, emotionally and, because of the geographic differences, logistically. What we have tried to do at Nebraska is build a team around the strengths of those players while helping to develop a player's "weakness" into a strength by the time they leave our program.

The longer I'm in the coaching profession, the more I realize it's more than the Xs and Os and the talent of the players on the field that win football games. There is a chemistry that must exist among the players—a feeling of togetherness, unity and unselfishness. When you combine that chemistry with knowledge of the game and talented athletes, you give yourself the best chance to win. Coach Osborne was a master at developing that chemistry.

Those who know Coach Osborne know him as a very caring person. As you hear from the players in this book, that becomes evident. Those who have come through the Nebraska football program also know when it came to handling discipline matters, that those matters were handled in a consistent, fair and impartial manner.

Nebraska fans are the best. The state is as unique as the football program. To that end, there is certainly a mirror-image effect between the fans and the program. A lot of fans identify so deeply with the principles that make both the state and the football program a success: hard work, perseverance and personal responsibility.

I am very fortunate to step into a job that has such great players, staff, support personnel, and, of course, fans. We will move forward into a new season. Yet, at the same time, we will never forget the eras of Bob Devaney and Tom Osborne. Enjoy the book.

His success is unparalleled. His record, 255 wins, just 49 losses and three ties, speaks for itself. The back-to-back national championships—and the three titles in four years (1994, '95, '97)—were a show of domination that college football will likely never see again.

But Tom Osborne's legacy is about much more than football. Osborne's December 10, 1997, announcement that he would step down as the University of Nebraska's head football coach sent shock waves throughout the nation.

Osborne was so much more than a coach, especially to those who played under him in Lincoln. Former players, who knew him far better than those outside the program—especially the media— have an affection for Osborne rarely seen in college athletics.

He was more than a coach to his players. Osborne was a father figure who was unrelenting in his support of his players and his demand for accountability and responsibility from those who strayed outside the rules. Unfortunately, because of the hit-man, attacking approach of the media in this day and age, the whole story rarely came out. On top of that, the information that did come out was often filled with inaccuracies and written with a detectable bias.

While Osborne dealt with the media in the most professional manner, his players took exception to the way he was treated. Many talk about their feelings in this book.

On a more positive note, those within Nebraska—and the various Nebraska clubs and organizations around the country— seldom doubted Osborne's handling of the situations.

Osborne is one of the most respected citizens in the Heartland. While almost all Husker fans will continue to support the program—and follow the team on the road—there is little doubt that those who love the Big Red also love Tom Osborne.

He was always calm and poised, even in the face of the biggest storm. The hearts of Nebraska fans broke when the Huskers came up just short of a national championship in the 1984 Orange Bowl, a 31-30 loss to Miami. We wanted the "good guy" to win. That feeling built to a new level in the late 1980s and early 1990s. The Huskers were always close to a national championship, but never quite cleared the final hurdle.

At the same time, Osborne just kept pushing forward. The deeply religious Osborne never wavered in his system and his undying belief in the "process."

The "process" is the biggest part of Osborne that will go unknown to those outside of Nebraska. Osborne truly enjoyed winning. However, the focus of his program was to bring young men in, help them develop personally, academically and athletically—and in a lot of cases, spiritually—and see them leave as better people, more often than not with a college degree.

That's why when Osborne said he didn't really "feel any different" the morning after beating Miami 24-17 and grabbing his first national crown in the 1995 Orange Bowl, many could not understand him: They wanted, or expected, Osborne to show emotion. But that national championship, and the one that followed with the 62-24 demolition of Florida in the 1996 Fiesta Bowl, were merely products of Osborne's process. The team changed in only one key way—it had more speed, especially in the defense—than ever before. The offensive line was still, for the most part, Nebraska-raised and corn-fed, beefing up in the outstanding NU weight training program. The walk-on program reached new levels, gaining national attention because players coming to pay their own way to school at Nebraska often turned down scholarship offers from other colleges. They chose, instead, to chase just about every Nebraska schoolboy's dream of running onto the field at Memorial Stadium as Nebraska's "third-largest city" roared its support.

The process never did change, it was only fine-tuned here and there. That's why, while there were scores of great athletes at Nebraska, there were very few superstars, especially compared to other highly-ranked college football teams. The national titles and high rankings were the product of players learning their roles, growing into those roles and then executing them on the football field. That was aided by a team chemistry few outside of the program ever understood and an affection for Osborne and his assistant coaches that rarely made headlines.

The outsiders did not often get to see the fairness with which Osborne treated the media. He admitted that talking to the media was not one of the favorite parts of his job, but just the same, he knew it was part of his responsibility. Being the role model that Osborne is, he dealt with the media professionally and with his "Golden Rule" approach: He almost always afforded those in the press far more respect than they returned.

While the media, even within Nebraska at times, claimed it was just doing its job, the criticism and cheap shots ran contrary to that. One player, who had been accused of shooting a man (the case was later dropped), was reported to be in jail on "second-degree murder" charges. The critical omission of "attempted" was corrected days later—if at all—in small print on an inside page, far away from the huge front-page headlines condemning the Huskers for allegations that, as it turned out, crumbled in a court of law. When the player in question was freed and the charges weren't pursued—that story didn't make the front page either. That is just one example of the sensationalism the media uses to take down those who are successful; an entire book could be written on what the national media did to Nebraska.

But in keeping with Osborne's "Golden Rule" approach to dealing with others, this book focuses on Coach Osborne's relationship with his players, what they felt when they first met him and how much he impacted their lives. Many of these stories, including the ones when players met Osborne during the recruiting process or in locker room chats, have not been told before now, or at least not as in-depth as presented here.

And you can be sure that other books on Osborne will follow. Some will have the whole story, most will likely not. However, as a supporter of what Coach Osborne stood for, and after hearing the way his players spoke about him, I will at least give those who want the truth the opportunity to hear it from those who actually played for Osborne and, more importantly, who grew up under Osborne's direction.

This is a book looking at the inside from the inside; it is the players telling the story.

To try to include all of Coach Osborne's former players in the book—even just the starters—would have taken away from the book's focus. Therefore, I included not just the star players—although many are included—but players who simply walked on at Nebraska and are in the business world now.

One of the truly amazing things that struck me was how almost all of the players, former and current, referred to Osborne as "Coach Osborne." None, even the ones well into their 30s, called him "Tom." Likewise, none referred to him only by his last name—it was, almost without exception, "Coach Osborne."

Also, the players who are now in the NFL were just incredibly easily accessible. Some said they welcomed the chance to talk about the University of Nebraska and Coach Osborne. In a lot of cases, they asked as many questions as I did: How's recruiting looking? How does the defense look? How is everyone, or a specific person? What was Senior Day like this year? The affection the players had for the program was quite apparent. The former Huskers in the NFL simply loved to talk about anything and everything having to do with Nebraska. A couple of players, when they found out I lived in western Nebraska, asked about the fishing and hunting. Dallas Cowboys linebacker Broderick Thomas asked about "the lake that Coach Osborne fished at out there—I remember him mentioning it." That place is Lake Minatare, and the fish are already nervous about Coach Osborne having more time on his hands.

Usually, when an interview is requested with an NFL player, the standard procedure is that a time is set up, and then the particular team's public relations staff calls the writer and hands the phone to the player. However, in several cases, the former Huskers took home my number and called in the evening. Broderick Thomas was one of those players. Likewise, New Orleans Saints end Jared Tomich said, "Call any time. It's good to hear how things are going in Nebraska. I really miss everyone."

I miss Jared, and the rest of the players, too.

And one more touch of Big Red-itis: The players in the NFL whom I interviewed asked who else I was talking to. The members of the classes of 1995 and 1996—the first two national championship teams—were especially interested in each other. Atlanta Falcons defensive back Michael Booker asked to pass a message along to Jamel Williams. After Williams was told of Booker's words, he asked who was next and was told Jared Tomich. Williams then asked that Tomich receive his greetings. When the message was relayed to Tomich, he asked who was going to be interviewed next. When told it was Zach Wiegert, Tomich had a message for him—and this went on and on for almost two dozen players. Mike McCashland, a defensive back for Osborne's 1983 team, asked if I was talking to Dean Steinkuhler. When told yes, McCashland asked if I'd extend an invitation to Steinkuhler from McCashland to go snowmobiling in Wyoming the first week in January 1998.

"You should see him go on a snowmobile," McCashland said with a laugh. "He's still about 320 pounds. There's not a snowmobile big enough. Have him call me if he'd like to go along."

Arizona center Aaron Graham talked about seeing Tomich the week before when the Cardinals played the Saints. Arizona's Dishman asked about how things were in Cozad (Nebraska). He talked glowingly about how he and his wife had just learned the previous week that their second child would be born in eight months. Dishman also asked me to pass the news along to his former teammates when I interviewed them. It was as much heartwarming as it was disarming, this genuine bond and affection the players share for the coaching staff, each other, the university and the entire state of Nebraska.

Almost every one of those players related that they stay in touch with each other. The topic of the phone calls? Not always NFL matters and not even "mostly" NFL stuff. Rather, Tomich and Booker confided that the players talk about Lincoln and the Big Red. One of the first topics to come up was when they will be returning to Lincoln. Whenever possible, they try to work it out so they can be in town at the same time.

While all of the former Huskers currently on NFL rosters make at least healthy six-figure salaries, they claim the greatest days of their lives were spent in Lincoln as members of the University of Nebraska football program. When they talked about the fans and the tunnel walk at Memorial Stadium, you could hear the emotion in their voices. All who were asked said they would give just about everything to be able to walk down that tunnel one more time as the roar of emotion from 76,000 fans in the sea of red pierced their eardrums but warmed their hearts.

Surely, several books about Osborne's era will follow in the coming months and years. While many will strike while the iron is hot, many of those will miss the mark. While this book might be the first to come out, it is important to note that some of the profits will go to Nebraska-based charity causes. While it was important to me to write this book, it was also important that part of the revenue generated from the purchase of this book by good, honest, hard-working people go to places that need it.

It is hard to fathom that we will no longer see Tom Osborne on the Nebraska sidelines. To that end, it is sad that we will not have a final home game to send him off.

Or is it?

Coach Osborne always wanted the attention to go to his players, assistant coaches and support staff. While he always made Senior Day special for those who had gone through his program, it is hard to imagine that he would have accepted having a day for himself. A man like Osborne would not likely have allowed himself to bask in the glory for he believes that glory is for God. He appreciated the effort but was not comfortable with the attention, which was evident while fireworks exploded over Memorial Stadium November 1, 1997 celebrating his 250th career win and a 69-7 victory over Oklahoma.

The sense of loss we feel from Osborne's departure is balanced only by the joy we must all feel knowing that he can finally spend some much-deserved time with his wife, children and grandchildren. Tom Osborne has long been a father figure to thousands, as fullback Joel Makovicka so eloquently stated at Osborne's resignation.

"It's been an emotional day for the players and for the coaches and for the whole state of Nebraska," Joel Makovicka said. "Sitting back there when Coach Osborne was saying he really didn't get a chance to see his kids grow up much, I just want to say he's had the chance to watch 150 guys on this team grow up and the thousands that came before us. He's been like a father figure to all of us in the values that he instills in us and the work ethic and his overall leadership."

Quarterback Scott Frost's words that day also carried a sense of bonding that is hard to imagine at other colleges and with other coaches.

"I'd just like to thank Coach Osborne—he has done a lot for me personally," Frost said. "He has done a lot of things that no one in college football has ever done. He's arguably the best coach in college football history. But the thing that he really does for his players—he just doesn't teach on the field, he leads by the example he sets. We don't just learn football around here. We learn how to be grown-ups, how to mature and how to be men. That's the thing that he has taught me the most."

So it seems more than fair that he take time for himself and his family. Both Osborne and his family certainly have earned it.

I would like to thank the current and former players for the time they gave me during interviews for this book. I am the kind of Nebraskan who will read just about anything about the Big Red. However, in this case, I wanted to make sure that I wrote a book for those who either truly care about Tom Osborne and the Huskers, or at least want to hear the side of the story that was often ignored, or misstated, by the media.

An era has ended in Lincoln. A man we had come to hold in such high regard has led the Big Red onto the field at Memorial Stadium for the last time. His calmness on the sidelines always made us feel like everything was in good hands and that all would end up all right. While we should have allowed ourselves the thought that his leaving would one day come, perhaps we just did not want to believe it ever would.

Frank Solich will take over the reins. Like Osborne, he has a great staff of assistant coaches. That was the one thing about this book that I hope does not go overlooked—the assistant coaches. All of the players interviewed mentioned them, to varying degrees. However, to keep the focus—and to keep the book from being a thousand pages—I reserved much of the space as a look back primarily at the impact Coach Osborne had on the players' lives. At the same time, I tried to give due respect and credit to an assistant coaching staff that is second to none.

I hope you enjoy what follows, and remember . . .

. . . GO BIG RED!

# CHAPTER 1

# MEETING
# COACH OSBORNE

*F*or those within Nebraska, the first memory of seeing Tom Osborne might be at Memorial Stadium. Perhaps it was in a picture in the newspaper. Maybe it was while he was speaking at a press conference or on television. Most fans will never forget Tom Osborne on the sideline, chewing his gum, wearing his headset, his calmness and poise belying the hard-hitting and emotional chaos on the field as 200- and 300-pound young men collided at frightening speeds.

For those who played for Osborne, the first contact they had with the coach came during recruiting season. Center Aaron Graham, who played at Nebraska from 1992-95, said he was working with a college recruiter, Jack Pierce, when Osborne called.

"It was tremendously exciting," Graham said. "Coach Osborne came down to Denton (Texas) to visit. He was taller than I thought—I had only seen him on TV. He was very tall. He just had an aura about him that made you feel calm and at ease. I was nervous, but once he started talking, it was easy."

While Graham had no doubts about Osborne's commitment to his players, what Osborne did next left an indelible mark on Graham.

"The thing I'll always remember, and be thankful for," Graham said, "is when I committed to them [the Huskers], I asked Coach Osborne, 'I don't want to put you out, but I would appreciate it if you could attend a signing party.' Looking back, I almost feel bad for even asking because he is so busy at that time of the year. But Coach Osborne didn't even hesitate. He said, 'It would be against NCAA rules for me to be at the signing, but I would love to come back the day after and maybe we can do something then.' So we had all my high school teammates, my closest friends and relatives, and had a celebration at my house. Coach Osborne got on a plane, flew himself down, got a rental car and drove to my house. He stayed for cake and ice cream, posed for pictures and shook hands with everyone there. That was almost his entire day. Looking back, that was right in the middle of recruiting season. It was the worst time for a guy like that to take a whole day out of his schedule. That meant so much to me—because to that point, it was the biggest day of my life."

Two time zones west and a world away from Lincoln, Brenden Stai said that something drew him to school in Lincoln.

"Even coming from California, I knew Nebraska received a lot of respect," Stai said. "Coach Osborne's a quality person and the Husker program has always had a lot of class. I took a visit there and met him—and that's all it took. I didn't know much about Nebraska, even after I visited—but I fell for Nebraska on that visit, hook, line and sinker. It was the best decision I ever made."

Marc Munford played for Heritage High School in Denver when Osborne recruited him. Munford later went on to be an All-American at Nebraska before playing for the Denver Broncos in the NFL.

"My father had played basketball with Coach Osborne for a team sponsored by Chubbeyville back in the 1960s," Munford said. "I asked my dad about Coach Osborne and he said Coach Osborne was always a straight shooter. They'd finish games and go to a bar in that town to have beer. My dad said Tom would walk in and have a vanilla milkshake wherever they went. So when he recruited me down in Denver, it was funny. Coach Osborne walks into the house, and my dad has a scotch and water. Coach Osborne walked in and said, 'Well, it's good to see things haven't changed.' My dad said, 'Hi Tom, you want a vanilla milkshake?' "

Munford, now an investment broker in Lincoln, had to be pinched that day, when Osborne showed up at his family's house in Denver, because it seemed like a dream.

"It was a neat feeling to be recruited by him," Munford said. "I was a little apprehensive, thinking he'd say, we don't want you.

That's just how it was, to see him in person. But it was a thrill to meet him."

Ken Graeber, who lettered three years (1982-84), said the first time he met Osborne, he was in awe, even though Osborne had only been on the job eight years when Graeber became a recruit.

"He wasn't quite as famous then because that was a long time ago," Graeber said. "But at that stage, you held him in higher esteem than you held the President of the United States when you shook his hand."

Ahman Green said, despite growing up in Omaha, he did not feel pressure from Osborne and the coaching staff to attend Nebraska.

"I first met him when he came to my house," Green said. "They were recruiting me. When I first talked to him, it was the first morning of recruiting day when coaches could get out and on the phone and start recruiting people. I knew it was coming. Still, it's a different thing when you live in Nebraska and you've got the top coach in college football calling your house. It's something that usually doesn't happen to the average player or person. It's just a great thing that happened and I took it from day-to-day with recruiting. When he came to my house for the first time, I got a good first impression of him. I knew he was a good coach, a player's coach. He told me they wanted me, no matter what, but it was up to me to make my decision."

Osborne's approach in recruiting Green left the biggest mark.

"He didn't come off like a salesman," Green said. "During recruitment, you feel like you're going out buying a car. You know, you are getting all these new sales pitches: 'You buy this car and it has this and that.' Coach Osborne just came out like a normal human being."

Bobby Newcombe, who in 1997 was one of the most sought-after option quarterbacks coming out of high school in New Mexico, already had heard plenty about Nebraska when Osborne started recruiting him.

"I knew a lot about Coach Osborne—like he's one of the

greatest college coaches ever," Newcombe said. "My first impression of him was that he was very down to earth. He never acted like he was the greatest coach ever. He just acted like he was . . . well, like he was Coach Osborne. He never had a big head on him."

Other college coaches talked about their programs to Green while Osborne simply told Green what was tangibly available at Nebraska.

"Coach Osborne was a big reason, because he wasn't trying to boast about Nebraska being this and that," Green said. "He just put it out in plain black-and-white. He told me what Nebraska expected out of me in terms of getting my education."

Three-time All-American rush end Grant Wistrom came to Lincoln from Webb City, Missouri, so he knew only a little about the Big Red fever that grips the state each year. And what he knew of Osborne was what he had read or seen on television.

"The first time I met him, it was the spring of my junior year in high school," Wistrom said. "It meant a great deal—I never grew up really a Nebraska fan, but I know how much this state cares for Nebraska football and I know how much Coach Osborne cares for us. They had been writing me letters and things like that. I decided to come up here and watch the spring football game. When I met him, the first thing that struck me was how tall he was. I mean, seeing the guy on TV, you never realize he's as tall as he is. I met him in the Hewit Center. We were eating or something. I could tell right away what a genuine person he was and what a sincere person he was.

"His mannerisms stand out. You can tell he's a person who cares about his players, cares about the people who work for him, and is concerned for basically everyone's welfare in general," Wistrom said. "I mean, even the janitors here talk about how nice he is. Not to say that they're 'just janitors,' but there are some people who might look down on them. Coach Osborne treats everybody with the same respect and dignity that they deserve.

"When I told him that I was going to come here, he said, 'Well, you know, we're excited to hear that and I hope things work out as well as we think they can for you,' " Wistrom said. "I knew what was expected of me coming up here: Work hard, be a good student, be a good person. I think that's what I've done. What I expected of them is everything I've gotten—just to be fair to me and treat me like a person, just take care of me in any way that's necessary.

"A great deal of why I came here was Coach Osborne," Wistrom said. "All the places I went to, I respected all the head coaches. The reason I came here may not have been Coach Osborne directly, but every organization takes on the characteristics of its leader. And Coach Osborne is the leader of this organization. Without a doubt, everybody here has the same type of attitude that he has. Everybody here treats you with respect. They are good people, and they honestly care about you. It may not have been the name 'Tom Osborne' that got me here, but it was his influence on the people that he hired, the choices that he makes and the decisions he makes that led me to come here."

Jason Peter, who came to Nebraska from Locust, New Jersey, said he could tell from his first interaction with Osborne that playing for the coach would be an experience like no other.

"Coach Osborne has a certain presence about himself," Peter said. "I mean, just talking to him on the phone, and then finally getting to meet with him—it's not like another head coach walking in and talking to you. When it's Coach Osborne, it's almost special. You feel privileged that you're one of the guys who he's talking to. I was certainly happy when they decided to recruit me."

While other coaches talked about football and academics, Osborne focused on academics and personal growth.

"He didn't even talk about football," Peter said. "He just talked about coming to Nebraska and more about just maturing as a person. That's one of the things that he's always stressed. Football doesn't mean the world to him. He'd rather see all of his players just succeed in the game of life. I remember that, especially, about him. A lot of coaches would come in and strictly talk football. With Coach Osborne, it was an entire, total package thing that he talked about."

Peter left Nebraska after the 1998 Orange Bowl as an All-American. However, Peter said the football field always took a backseat to the classroom. And because of that attitude, he left the University with his degree in tow, graduating in December 1997.

"Coach Osborne told me that he felt I could come in and I could eventually help this program out," Peter said. "He was happy that I was coming, and I was happy that I was coming and getting the chance to play for Coach Osborne. Of course, he told me academics were first and that was my first priority—to make sure things were done in the classroom. Then, you get the opportunity to play on the field. That's one thing that Coach Osborne told me when I committed to come to Nebraska."

Matt Davison, a freshman on the 1997 NU team, said Osborne came to a game at his school during prep basketball season.

"Coach Osborne came to a basketball game my senior year of high school," Davison said. "It wasn't the first time I met him. But it was the first time he came to my hometown to see me. I just remember the respect that he got by just walking into the building and how he carried himself with such composure. From that moment, it told me what kind of man he was. He just told me what he tells everybody: They recruit good athletes and guys who have good character. He thought that I fit the mold of a Nebraska football player. When he told me that, it gave me a lot of confidence coming to a program like this. Hearing it from a guy that I respected so much was really important.

"When I accepted the scholarship, I was talking to Coach Osborne on the phone," Davison said. "He said that no matter what happens from here on out, I have a scholarship to the University of Nebraska. This is before I even signed. Growing up in this state, from the time you're old enough to watch the games or understand, everybody is talking about Coach Osborne. The program is pretty much built around him. He creates the whole attitude and the character of this whole team. There is so much respect for this program, that he had a big part in my decision to come here."

As with other players, All-American offensive lineman Aaron Taylor saw Osborne's honesty during their first face-to-face visit.

"I met Coach Osborne on the trip when I came up here to visit," Taylor said. "I heard a lot about him through Coach [Milt] Tenopir, who was recruiting me. But my first contact with Coach Osborne was up here. He came across to me as a real honest man, straightforward, gentle, kind and I liked that—I really liked that about him. I liked the way he went about the whole thing. That's what I was looking for, a lot of honesty from a guy. And he gave me that. It was exciting to see."

While the few players who have gotten into trouble have gained most of the attention from the media, Taylor said the team is proud to have so many positive role models. And he gives all the credit for that to Osborne.

"Coach Osborne said he expected a lot of things from me—to do good in school, to give everything I have out there on the field," Taylor said. "He didn't say, 'You know, I want you to go out and be the best player out there,' and what not. He just said he expected a lot of hard work out of me and to be a good role model. I think I've done all that and I definitely don't want to let him down in that area. He was a big reason why I chose Nebraska. He was everything I wanted in a coach. He was honest and down to earth and a great coach. That's the biggest reason why I came here—I guess he really is THE reason why I came here."

And Taylor didn't disappoint. He finished his career as a Husker having been named an All-American in 1996 and 1997, as well as receiving the 1997 Outland Trophy, an award that recognizes college football's top interior lineman.

Scott Frost went through some tough times during his college career. Husker fans may have felt scorned when he chose Stanford over Nebraska. Yet when Bill Walsh left as Stanford's coach and Frost wanted to leave, he knew Nebraska never abandoned him, even though he did not choose Nebraska when he came out of Wood River High School.

"When a lot of people were doubting me and a lot of people were down on me, even after I went out to another school, he was always there for me," Frost said. "He never backed down that I could be a quarterback and play here. And you know, I owe a lot to him. I think the whole team feels that way."

Sheldon Jackson said the initial appeal of the program was the winning tradition. However, Jackson admitted that once he met Osborne, he did not need to visit with any other coaches.

"Of course, there was the glamour of the program, as far as being up there and having national prominence around the country," Jackson said. "But his overall genuineness was evident to us, and that's why I came here."

Joel Makovicka's older brother, Jeff, was a fullback on both of the Huskers' national championship teams. Still, Joel needed some time to get over the initial shock of finally meeting with Osborne and realizing he was going to play for the Huskers.

"It was a thing where my brother played here, so he knew who I was," Joel Makovicka said. "But it's still the kind of thing where you're really intimidated the first time you talk to him—he's a legend around the state. Growing up, you just watch Nebraska football and Coach Osborne. When you get to talk to him, it's kind of an intimidating experience until you get to know him. Once you get to know him, he becomes easier and easier to talk to."

Osborne's affection for his players was apparent from the outset.

"He seemed so genuine and sincere," Joel Makovicka said. "He's really soft-spoken and has a real unique sense of humor."

Toby Wright was a junior college All-American at Phoenix College and had a chance to go to several Pac-10 powerhouse colleges. He didn't think Nebraska was one of his options until one day in his junior college coach's office.

"The first time I spoke to Coach Osborne, I was at junior college," Wright said. "My coach said he knew someone who knew Coach Osborne. My juco coach said, 'I know other schools are interested in you, but what would you say if I told you I could get you into Nebraska?' I was like, 'Really?' I got a call from Coach Osborne. It was incredible. All the coaches from USC, UCLA and other schools called, but it wasn't the same. When Coach Osborne called my house, I didn't really react—I just froze. My mom answered the phone and said, 'It's Coach Osborne from Nebraska.' I was like, 'What?' I grabbed the phone and just had to hold it for a minute because I was so nervous."

After talking to Osborne and visiting Nebraska, Wright canceled visits to other schools.

"Nebraska was my first visit," Wright said. "I didn't bother to go anywhere else. Especially with me coming from Arizona, I was definitely thinking about coming back to the West Coast. His sincerity made it very comfortable for me there [in Nebraska] right away."

Like Toby Wright, Troy Dumas said Osborne first contacted him by telephone.

"I couldn't believe it—that I was actually talking to him," Dumas said. "That was the first college coach I ever talked to, and I was just doing cartwheels. I didn't visit any other college after meeting Coach Osborne and visiting Nebraska. Once I met Coach, that was what I went on for my decision—I was sold."

Zach Wiegert was a highly-recruited lineman coming out of high school in Fremont. Like other Nebraskans, Wiegert was pretty sure that, if given the opportunity, he'd become a Husker.

"He called me on the phone and said, 'Zach, would you like a scholarship?' " Wiegert recalled. "He had been to our house when he recruited my brother. The only other place I considered was Washington, because they offered me a scholarship before Nebraska did. My mom had been thinking about moving to Seattle, so that was a factor. But growing up in Nebraska and everything . . . once Nebraska offered, that was it for me."

Former Nebraska All-American Dave Rimington, who played from 1979-82, said he was surprised when Osborne called to recruit him.

"The first time I spoke with him was on the telephone," Rimington said. "I was a senior in high school and our team had just played our first game of the season. Coach Osborne offered me a scholarship."

A Husker fan, Rimington knew about the tradition at Nebraska, but had yet to venture to Memorial Stadium.

"I had never gone to a Nebraska game and I was very nervous," Rimington said. "I grew up with the whole Nebraska mystique when Bob Devaney was the coach. I followed when Coach Osborne took over."

Steve Forch (1984-85, '87) was a native of Lincoln, and said it seemed too good to be true when he was offered a scholarship.

"Coach Osborne offered a scholarship, which I immediately accepted," Forch said. "There wasn't much thought about it for me—it was overwhelming. It was like, 'Really, you're kidding me.' Of course, Coach Osborne's son, Mike, played with me at Lincoln East High School, so I had a little exposure to him. I grew up in Lincoln so I knew him from church—we went to the same church. He was always Tom Osborne, the coach, the man."

Heisman Trophy winner Mike Rozier, who went on to play in the NFL for the Houston Oilers and Atlanta Falcons, said Osborne is about much more than football.

"In addition to being a good coach," Rozier said, "he is a good man. He has always treated me fairly and treated all of the players who want to work and play hard, the same way."

Mark Daum was a Husker that traveled one of the longest distances of any in-state player to Lincoln.

"For me personally, he made me feel really comfortable," said Daum, who led the Huskers in tackles for losses, with nine, in 1983, as a linebacker. Daum saved the correspondence from Osborne which he received while in high school.

"I went to some of the summer football camps, and that's how I first met Coach Osborne," Daum said. "He started contacting me through letters. I saved a lot of that stuff. My senior year, he didn't give me a scholarship but really wanted me to walk on. That's all the opportunity I could have asked for and it worked out great."

Although he attended several NU football camps growing up in Nebraska, former Husker John Parrella did not really get to know Osborne until he enrolled at NU.

"I felt, of course, respect, knowing I was talking to someone of that profile and standing," Parrella said. "Being as young as I was, the respect factor was really high. When I first met him in person, I was as nervous as you can imagine. I had seen him at football camps that I went to when I was in high school. Then, my senior year, I talked to him about going there. He basically just said 'hi,' and that he'd watch me during the season. Each time I got to talk to him was very special."

Rimington, a two-time Academic All-American, also knew about Osborne, but still was unprepared for the first phone call from the coach.

"I knew everything about him. I was just in shock that he offered me a scholarship," Rimington said. "I had broken my leg the year before, so I was just excited they had that kind of confidence that I could play for them. I played it coy, said I'd go on a few recruiting trips. Eventually, I obviously accepted the scholarship. Coach Osborne still gives me grief about that and we still laugh about it."

As was the case with any Nebraska recruit, Osborne talked first about academics.

"I was awe-struck with the whole program," said Rimington, who graduated the season before Osborne took over for Bob Devaney as head coach. "Coach Osborne looked into my parents' eyes and said, 'If Dave comes to Nebraska, he will always have a scholarship.' That was important, because I had just broken my leg the year before, and we knew there were no guarantees at a lot of colleges. But Coach Osborne told my parents, 'We won't pull a scholarship if a guy gets hurt. The only way we'd ever pull it is if he didn't give the effort.' "

For other native Nebraska sons like Cory Schlesinger, the chance to play for Coach Osborne and the Big Red was the realization of a childhood dream.

"I was recruited mainly by Coach [Dan] Young," Schlesinger said. "I first met Coach Osborne when I visited the campus. The first thing that struck me was the honesty you could feel just being around him. Coach Osborne was a huge reason why I chose Nebraska. At the same time, I was from Nebraska, so when I had the opportunity to go there, it wasn't a tough decision."

Michael Booker was in southern California when Osborne said he would like to visit Booker's house with Assistant Coach Ron Brown.

"I was shocked when Coach Osborne and [assistant coach] Ron Brown said they were coming to my house to recruit me," Michael Booker said. "To my house? In California? People don't seem to like to come to California as it is, and I was going to believe Tom Osborne was going to come to my house?"

Booker expected to be in awe of Osborne—which he was, to a degree. But what caught Booker and his mother off-guard was that Osborne did not come across as a football coach as much as he did an educator.

"Coach Osborne came over and he was just so humble," Booker said. "He wasn't flashing any Big Eight championship rings or anything like that. He and Coach Brown talked to my mother and won her over right away. The moment they left the house I knew I was going to Nebraska."

Tony Veland, who was drafted in the sixth round by the Denver Broncos in 1996 after helping the Huskers to back-to-back national titles, went to Omaha Benson High School. While he always dreamed of playing for the Huskers, he did not know if Nebraska would be interested in him.

"I didn't think Nebraska would recruit me," Veland said. "When I met him, I could see the honesty up front and that he really cared about kids. To be honest, Coach Osborne was THE reason I chose Nebraska."

Because of questions surrounding his academic performance in high school, Jared Tomich, who later was drafted by the New Orleans Saints after helping the Huskers to back-to-back national titles, was not heavily pursued by colleges. The interest shown by Husker Defensive Coordinator Charlie McBride was as welcome as it was unexpected by Tomich as he finished high school in Indiana.

"I wasn't really recruited by anyone else besides Nebraska, except the University of Cincinnati," Tomich said. "When I visited Nebraska, Coach McBride was the one who had been recruiting me.

But I got to meet Coach Osborne during my visit. It was incredible. He is one of those people who just have an aura about them. [Saints coach Mike] Ditka is a lot that way, too—you just feel something when you are around him. With Coach Osborne, you could tell who he was and what he was about when you first met him. You just fed off of it. You can sense the tremendous character he has."

An All-State running back in high school in Indiana, Jamel Williams, who played a key role in the Huskers' repeat as national champions, said he knew Osborne would make sure his players were taken care of at NU.

"I was still in high school in Indiana, and Coach Osborne called," Williams said. "He came down and visited me at my school. The first thing you can tell about Coach Osborne when you meet him is that he's very honest. He is like a father figure."

Williams, who was playing for the Washington Redskins in 1997, said he was impressed with Osborne's sincerity after their first conversation.

"He was a big reason I chose Nebraska," Williams said. "He was just so straightforward. There was nothing phony about him. You know how you can see how a lot of people have a part of them that is sort of phony? That's not Coach Osborne. Not a single part of him is phony."

Tony Veland, who began his Husker career as a quarterback but later moved to the defensive backfield, was impressed when he was recruited by Osborne. Although Nebraska's winning tradition gets a lot of publicity nationwide, Veland said he knew from his first meeting with Osborne that football was just part of the whole process of being a student at the University of Nebraska.

"The thing about it is that Coach Osborne was about so much more than winning football games," Veland said. "He enjoyed winning, but Coach's big thing was to help boys grow into men, not just be good football players. A lot of coaches just aren't that way."

Because of academic shortcomings, Booker knew he would not be able to play immediately at Nebraska. However, Osborne was very methodical in talking about the academic process, making sure

Booker understood up front that there would be no football without Booker first attaining the academic requirements to be eligible.

"It's just like going upstairs," Booker said. "To reach the top, you have to take the first step, and then the next one, and so on. It's the same thing for college football. Those of us who were 'props' had to take it even more seriously that we were students first and athletes second."

Tomich was also a casualty of Proposition 48, but he knew right away that Osborne was about school much more than football.

"The big thing for me was grades, because I was a 'prop' and wasn't eligible when I first got there," Tomich said. "Coach Osborne sat down with me and told me I had to get my grades. He said, 'That is all I expect from you. After that, we'll take the next step.' No one had really talked to me about football because my academic background wasn't strong. I'll keep that memory for a lifetime."

John Parrella, a native of Grand Island, said Osborne made it clear at the outset that football would come second to academics.

"Coach Osborne always talked about, that to be a good football player, first you had to do well in school," Parrella said. "He made it available for us to develop some kind of faith in the Lord. To say that meant a lot to guys on the team. It's not just lifting weights and studying—it's the complete development and trying to reach your potential in everything in your life."

Dallas Cowboys linebacker Broderick Thomas said he felt a sense of pride every time he saw Osborne help a current or former Husker.

"To see him deal with so many guys the way he did, makes you see how much he loved all of his players," Thomas said. "Doug DuBose needed help, and Coach Osborne helped him secure control of his life. Other coaches would have said, 'You're off the team—that's it.' Coach Osborne tried to make a good life for them and it didn't have much to do with football in a lot of cases. He would help any player, from a starter to a walk-on who never even got into a game. He always made people see the positive as being possible during negative times. I've seen him extend his hand so much. His expertise at fatherhood showed what a great dad he was. Other coaches would say, 'That's enough, leave.' But not our coach."

Thomas said Tampa Bay Coach Tony Dungy is the only other coach that has made a similar impression on him.

"What sticks out for me is that Coach Osborne, as quiet and humble as he is, at the same time, is stern and powerful," Thomas said. "The only one who reminds me of that is Tony Dungy, who was the defensive coordinator in Minnesota when I was there. The expertise and football brilliance . . . a humble person who puts God first, just like Coach Osborne. Those are two of the best football people—and just the plain best people, period—who I've ever been around."

Chris Dishman remembers attending a camp in Lincoln after his freshman year in high school in Cozad. He saw Rob Zatechka, who was a two-time Academic All-American selection while at Nebraska, in an elevator.

"Rob said, 'Coach Osborne called me. I've got a scholarship to Nebraska,' " Dishman recalled. "I said, 'Wow, Coach Osborne called you?' I thought about how cool that would be. That year, I told my parents I wanted to go to the camp. Coach Osborne talked to me a little. The next year, they liked me and I was offered a scholarship. I'm from Cozad, so I grew up in Nebraska. For me, it was a dream come true."

# CHAPTER 2

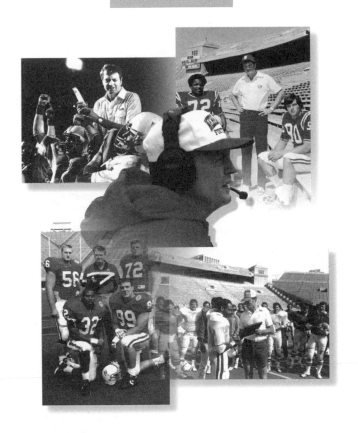

# NO STAR POWER
# IN NU'S UNIVERSE

$W$hat keeps a lot of players in the program and striving to get more playing time is that Osborne values all players equally.

"He thinks we all are important," Joel Makovicka said. "He always talks about the scout team being important every week. That's how we prepare to go out and play well. If it wasn't for the scout team, we wouldn't play as well. Coach Osborne feels like everyone is important."

An All-State selection at Omaha Central High School, Ahman Green said he knew he would get no special treatment at Nebraska.

"He said I should expect to get pushed in practice," Green said. "If I messed up, he was going to tell me when I messed up. And the other coaches, like Coach Solich, told me the same thing—they'd treat me fairly, I wouldn't get treated differently because I was a freshman. I would get a fair shot at whatever position I was at."

Defensive back Mike Minter was highly recruited out of high school and would go on to earn scores of conference honors for the Huskers before starting as a rookie in the NFL for the Carolina Panthers. But Minter said there was no such thing as "star treatment" in Lincoln, even for the highest profile recruits.

"You could be a starter or on the scout team, and it would not matter. Coach Osborne believes in treating everyone the same." Minter said.

Adam Treu knew all about the Huskers as a native of Lincoln. However, he was still struck hard by reality when he joined the Big Red.

"When I was a redshirt freshman, I didn't work that hard in practice," Treu said. "I was All-State in high school, so I was used to playing a lot. I came to Nebraska that first year and had a pessimistic attitude because I thought I was supposed to be good. But everyone at Nebraska is good. Coach Osborne told me that I'd have to wait my turn like anyone else, unless you are a real standout."

That experience led Treu to realize that the playing field—in this case, the opportunity to play—depended only on effort and execution, not a sort of prep football resumé.

"It's tremendous how they give everyone an equal chance," Treu said. "And it is not often that you see animosity between the players who are starting and those who are pushing them."

Osborne promises neither a position nor playing time. The only guarantee is that if the player shows a commitment, so will the university and coaches.

"He doesn't make promises to anyone," Tom Rathman said. "Coming out of high school, you see all the blue chippers they get in Lincoln. You think, 'Do I even have a chance, an opportunity?' You have to go out on the football field and play hard. I'm talking every play in practice even."

The lack of star treatment in the program is something that leaves an impression on all players, especially in-state players who perhaps aren't heavily recruited by other colleges.

"He didn't try to sell me anything, no promises or anything like that," Green said. "He just told me, 'If you come here, we don't know where you'll be at on the depth chart. We just want you. If you come here, give it all you've got. I'm not guaranteeing you a starting spot.' He told me everything straight up and was real honest with me. Out of all of the college coaches who recruited me, he was the most down-to-earth coach."

Coaches at other colleges told Toby Wright he would be an immediate starter; Osborne did not.

"One thing that stuck out for me is that he never guaranteed me anything when it came to playing time and that kind of thing," Wright said. "He said, 'If you come in and work hard, everything will be there for you and you'll have a chance to excel in the classroom and on the field.' "

Coming from East Butler High School in Brainard, Nebraska, Joel Makovicka knew the special opportunity afforded walk-ons in Lincoln.

"I played 8-man football and was from a small school," Makovicka said. "He said as far as me walking on, it was a great place to come and play. It's a place where they don't treat walk-ons any different. You're part of the team and they give you a fair shake. It's just something he stands by. All the players respect that. Nebraska is a unique institution. They rely heavily on their walk-on program—and that's what keeps it rolling. Whether you are starting and an All-American, or if you are on the scout team, his feelings toward you don't change."

Many coaches told Aaron Taylor he could start right away at their schools. Not Osborne.

"It was a situation where he said, 'We think you're a good football player. You can do a lot of good things here, but it has to come through hard work,'" Taylor said. "I respected that. You know, a lot of coaches will tell you, 'You are the greatest football player in the world. You can come up here and start right away.' Coach Osborne was like, 'Well, it's going to take a lot of hard work and we think you can do it.' That's what I liked about him."

Mark Daum said recruits from even the smallest high schools felt like the playing field was always level when it came to the opportunity to play in Lincoln.

"I was at Dix High School in western Nebraska playing 8-man football. Coach Osborne did not make me feel, in any way, intimidated. He made me feel like the sky was the limit—that it was all up to me. He gave me a lot of inspiration."

Bobby Newcombe played a lot as a true freshman on Osborne's final team in 1997.

"He told me I could expect a lot of support from all the coaches and all the academic facilities around here," Newcombe said. "From me, they only expect that I give it all I have on the field and in the classroom. Coach Osborne never promised anything to anybody, unless he was sure of it. That's the great thing about him; he won't lie to anybody. He'll tell you what he knows. He told me that if I work hard, and I come in ready to play and I build my confidence, then I'd have a shot at playing. He said, depending on my attitude and the way I worked, I'd have a pretty good future here."

Steve Forch, who played for NU some 15 years before Newcombe came to Lincoln, nonetheless, has a similar memory.

"Coach Osborne was very fair, I thought," Forch said. "He was straight with you. There were no mental games. He let his assistant coaches do their own things. That contributed to the success."

Grant Wistrom knows he was far more than just a number in Lincoln under Osborne.

"He remembers the names of just about every player that has ever played here—walk-ons to All-Americans—and I think that says a lot about him," Wistrom said. "You can say it until you're blue in the face, but until you've played here and played under him, you know the man but you really don't know how much he cares about you. Everybody knows if they have a problem they can go to Coach Osborne and he's going to do everything he can to help them out."

Terry Connealy went from playing 8-man football for Hyannis High School in western Nebraska to gaining All-Big 8 honors for the Huskers as a defensive tackle. He said the players knew the rules were the same for everyone.

"That's just the kind of guy Coach Osborne is," Connealy said. "It didn't matter if the player was last or first on the depth chart. He took serious interest in every one of us."

Mark Blazek knew some of the recruits in his class were getting looked at by dozens of major college powerhouses. While Blazek was an in-state kid just looking for a shot, he said Osborne made him feel right at home.

"The biggest impression for me was the first on-campus recruiting visit," Blazek said. "I sat in his office with my folks. He talked to me the same way he would an All-American high school kid from Texas who was being recruited by 10 or 12 schools."

Sheldon Jackson had high hopes when he came to Nebraska. However, he knew that even a scholarship player such as himself had to earn his stripes.

"Coach Osborne treats everybody equally," Jackson said. "He gives everybody a chance. Not only does he preach being good and doing what's right, he also lives his life that way. Players can see him doing what he actually preaches, so it carries over more and has more of an impact than just preaching it would have."

Although some colleges proudly point out that they have more players in the NFL than Nebraska, Blazek said, that in itself is a credit to the Huskers and Osborne.

"We may not have as many players in the NFL as some colleges, but that just all the more shows what kind of a coach he is," Blazek said. "Historically, we don't have the best recruiting classes. Very seldom are we No. 1, 2, 3, 4 or 5 in recruiting classes. But somehow, we manage to be No. 1, 2 or 3 in the polls each year. A lot of the in-state kids they recruit aren't highly touted and aren't recruited by UCLA, the Florida schools, the Texas schools or the West Coast schools, yet they come here and contribute. Nebraska has been able to maintain a program that is unique in the country because they bring in so many local kids and not as many nationally touted players. But those Nebraska kids get in the system and, if they work hard, become an important part of the team."

"He treats everyone fair," said Matt Davison, a freshman wide receiver on the 1997 team, "from the scout team to the starting quarterback."

# CHAPTER 3

# GOING OUT
# ON TOP

*I*t was, to many, a fitting ending.

The man regarded as the best coach ever, heading toward retirement at the top of the heap, with a third national championship—in only four years—in tow was ready to complete an era of excellence.

A happy ending to those who really, truly appreciated Tom Osborne. Not just that his team had gone 13-0. Not just that the Huskers had pounded the No. 3 team in the nation, Tennessee, 42-17, including a late, mop-up touchdown that came long after the game had been decided. At that time, substitutes were manning the defensive line as All-Americans Grant Wistrom and Jason Peter worried about a different plan of attack; how to get Coach Osborne with an icy cold "Gatorade bath," which on this night, consisted of ice water.

"We wanted to make a statement by the way we played," said NU offensive lineman Aaron Taylor. "I think we did that. We came through this season undefeated for Coach Osborne."

And—surprise—Osborne was not overly emotional after coaching his final game.

"I could hear his voice crack now and then, but it wasn't like you'd expect," Taylor said. "He got a little emotional and told us, 'Thanks for everything.' He was a little emotional, but it was a typical post-game speech."

Ahman Green, who announced the following week that he would forego his final year of eligibility to enter the NFL, said Osborne was still reserved after the Orange Bowl.

"He was poised, as usual," Green said. "He gave us his usual pep talk. He told us he loved coaching us, he loved the coaches he coached with over the past 25 years. And to give him a win like this . . . he just couldn't put it into words."

To the coaches who voted Nebraska a much-deserved share of the national championship, it was a fair ending, one that Osborne and his Huskers earned—this was no charity drive to get the Big Red a share of the national title.

Call it what you might—a happy, fair or fitting ending.

But the truth is this: The way things unfolded was the only possible ending for the man who symbolized what the Heartland has always been about. He leaves as a coaching legend to most, if not all, in the world of college football.

To Nebraskans everywhere Tom Osborne has been that and so much more.

Sure, the Huskers have a third national title in four years.

Sure, the Huskers have gone undefeated three times in four years, compiling a 60-3 mark along the way, and had been within a field goal in 1993 and a botched fourth-down defense in the Big 12 Championship game of 1996, of being conceivably the five-time defending national champions.

But it is about so much more than that. It is about hard work and standing up for what is right—not necessarily for what is popular. It is about having an unshakeable faith, in both the Lord and the human spirit. It is about redemption and responsibility.

The final season, like the 24 others under Osborne, was about life as much as it ever was about football. Society is often portrayed as a ship spinning wildly out of control, morally and spiritually. Yet with Osborne at the wheel of the good ship Nebraska, we knew it would stay on course. Big Red football represents so much more than just the gridiron to Nebraskans. It's about hard work, counting on your neighbor, always being there for the ones you love, dealing with adversity, having faith and knowing that if you do your best and help those around you, everything will—one way or another—simply turn out all right.

When the ESPN/USA Today Coaches Poll was released, it listed Nebraska as National Champion in the wee hours of the morning of Saturday, January 3, 1998.

After Washington State had put on an impressive performance

and eventually lost to Michigan, 21-16, the Huskers, ranked No. 2, had to be impressive against No. 3 Tennessee in the FedEx Orange Bowl.

Nebraska was impressive and more. The numbers—not unlike Osborne's final record of 255-49-3 over 25 years—are mind-boggling. Nebraska rushed for 409 yards against one of the top defenses in the nation. Peyton Manning, second in the Heisman voting this year—and the certain top pick in the NFL Draft had he entered it last year—was held to 134 yards passing. The Volunteers rushed for only 128 yards.

So Nebraska lived up to its billing and then earned top billing in the ESPN/USA Today Coaches Poll as well.

"Every time we went out on that field tonight, we knew we were playing for [Coach Osborne]," Peter told reporters after the game. "We could see it in his eyes that this game was different."

Different—and with a sense of finality to it that most Nebraskans were dreading—Osborne's last game on the sideline guiding the Huskers.

"When you go 13-0 and have the year we had," Osborne said, "you hope some recognition would come."

It did. A national title—wait, make that ANOTHER national title. Even the national media seemed to sense that the title was deserved.

"Justice was done," ESPN's Kirk Herbstreit said. "Without a doubt, [Nebraska] deserved a split championship."

"Without a doubt?" There never were any doubts with Osborne running the show.

"This was not a vote against Michigan," said ESPN analyst Lee Corso. "It was a vote for Nebraska."

As Pittsburgh Steelers offensive lineman Brenden Stai, a guard on the "Pipeline" team that won Osborne's first national title in 1994, watched the 1998 Orange Bowl, he wondered if incoming coach Frank Solich would have enough experience in the offensive line for the upcoming season.

"I was kind of worried about them for next year because they're losing a lot of guys in the line," Stai said. "But then, in the Orange Bowl against Tennessee, we had third and fourth stringers in there, and we're still knocking Tennessee around. I was so excited to see them kick Tennessee. There's a few guys here [on the Steelers] from Tennessee, so I really enjoyed the game. We wore them down in the second half—sound familiar?"

At the celebration, held at the Devaney Center in Lincoln the afternoon after Nebraska beat Tennessee and was named national champions, the Husker faithful gathered one final time under Coach Osborne.

"Everyone knows we have the best coach in the history of college football," Grant Wistrom said on a tape made that morning and played at the Devaney Center because Wistrom had stayed behind in Miami. "With our new coach, we're going to keep steamrolling people and racking up national championships."

Always showing the same class in victory that he showed during those New Year's Day defeats, Osborne expressed happiness for, of all folks, Michigan.

"It certainly is very gratifying—from our standpoint, it couldn't have worked out any better," Osborne said. "I'm really pleased for the University of Michigan, strangely enough. They very much deserve to be national champions. I thought we did, too."

Just as he was when the Huskers lost the national championship to Miami in the 1984 Orange Bowl, and as he was when the Huskers won the national title over Miami in the 1995 Orange Bowl and demolished Florida for the crown in the 1996 Fiesta Bowl, Osborne showed little emotion about his third national championship.

That might surprise some, but it did not surprise any Nebraskan. Because, like a farmer, Osborne knows that an "up" could well be followed by a "down" and vice versa. He kept an even keel because that is who he always has been, celebrating the power of the human spirit in his ho-hum way because he has always been more concerned with players reaching their spiritual, personal, academic and athletic potential than he ever was with trophies and titles.

He will not disappear entirely. You can count on seeing his face in regard to his many charitable efforts. He is a Nebraskan—this is where he is from, and part of who he is—so he won't be giving up the rows of cornfields and plains for bright lights and a big city.

Still, in the shadows of one of the most memorable moments for Nebraska football, there is a somber atmosphere as Osborne jogs from the sideline to the locker room for a final time. Frank Solich will be a good—maybe great—coach for the Huskers. And we all know the cupboard is never bare in Lincoln.

There are high school student-athletes playing 8-man football in the most remote outposts of Nebraska who will one day play in a national championship game for the University of Nebraska. The walk-on program will continue to be the best in the nation. Places like Wood River, East Butler, North Platte, Hyannis, Waverly, Columbus, Scottsbluff, Kearney and Grand Island, in addition to the metro areas of Lincoln and Omaha, will continue to send their young men to Lincoln to get a top-notch education and wear the white helmets with the red "N" on the sides.

Colleges nationwide will continue to try to build their football programs in the image that Bob Devaney and Tom Osborne built Nebraska. They will come close at times, but when the final polls are out, 95 to 100 percent of them will be in the Big Red's rearview mirror. The legacy of Tom Osborne will never be forgotten.

But we will push ahead, learning from yesterday and planning for tomorrow, while enjoying the present, because it has been such a great place to be during the Osborne era.

The win over Tennessee was a great ending to Osborne's tenure. It is a good beginning to Coach Solich's reign. And, in these parts, we always welcome—and, really, have come to expect—the national championship trophies.

It was a fitting ending. A fair ending. A happy ending.

To be sure, it was the only ending for the Tom Osborne era.

# CHAPTER 4

# BACK-TO-BACK
# NATIONAL
# CHAMPIONSHIPS

*A*ll of the players recruited to Nebraska in the early 1990s knew about the Huskers' successes. They also knew that Osborne had yet to win a national championship, despite the fact that the Big Red was in the hunt on practically a yearly basis.

When Osborne won his first national title with a 24-17 win over Miami in the Orange Bowl in 1995, the players took as much pride in helping Osborne win his first title as they did in their own personal accomplishment of being national champions.

"It's hard to put it into words," Jared Tomich said. "For all the years and years he had coached, he hadn't won a national championship. Even though he was almost always close to getting it, he could never quite win one. But Coach had given so much to all of us. He helped us grow. To give him a national championship was special, but it can't compare to what he gave us as young men."

Detroit Lions fullback Cory Schlesinger said he can't recall any kind of championship, in any sport, meaning more than Osborne's first national championship.

"To win that first national championship meant a lot to a whole lot of different people—Coach Osborne, the assistant coaches, all the guys playing and the whole state of Nebraska," Schlesinger said.

Aaron Graham, an All-American center on the 1995 squad, said the first national title was for Osborne personally, and the second was to ensure Osborne's legacy—especially the manner in which the Huskers won over Florida.

"The first one was definitely a monkey-off-the-back type of deal," Graham said. "The second one was, almost for a lack of a better term, a demonstration of dominance. We didn't want people to say that Coach Osborne just had a team that was good enough to finally win a single national championship. The second was important because it showed this was a program worthy of several national championships."

Tony Veland said the back-to-back titles were rewards a long time in coming for Osborne, who had been slapped with a reputation of being able to win any and every game—except the big one, when it mattered most.

"It meant a lot to me," Veland said. "Coach Osborne put his whole heart into the program. For all he had accomplished before I got there, the big game had eluded him. He got a bad reputation for not being able to win the big game. So when we won it, it was doubly nice. First, it was great for the players to bring the University of Nebraska, the state and the fans a national championship. Second, it got that reputation of Coach Osborne not being able to win the big game erased."

The players who were on the roster for the national championships are proud they were able to send Osborne out with a trio of national titles.

"It means a lot to me to have played on the national championship teams Coach Osborne had," Jason Peter said. "It's sad that Coach Osborne is leaving. But I'm glad that I'm able to play in the last game he coaches. But being part of his national championship teams means a lot. People always look back on those teams in 1994 and '95 [and '97], and I'll be able to say that I was part of it. I'm thrilled about that."

While Osborne never showed a lot of emotion over winning national championships, Peter said all the players know the titles were special for Osborne.

"I'm sure they mean a lot to him," Peter said. "People were giving him a hard time, five or six years ago, about not being able to win the big games and stuff like that. You knew it was just a matter of time and Coach Osborne deserved them. He's the greatest coach in the country and one of the best coaches ever. It was very gratifying to everyone on the team, and even just the people in the state of Nebraska, for Coach Osborne to get those national titles. As much as he downplays it, I'm sure it means a lot to him."

To win the first national title and follow it up with a second consecutive national championship left the players believing that Osborne was finally getting the respect he had long deserved as a college coach.

"It was a great thrill to be a part of the team when Coach Osborne won his first national championship," Michael Booker said. "We felt Coach Osborne deserved a national championship. To be a part of that, and then to be a part of winning back-to-back national championships after we beat Florida in the Fiesta Bowl, really means a lot."

To beat Florida that badly was simply a product of Osborne and the rest of the coaching staff paying attention to detail, according to Fiesta Bowl Most Valuable Player Tommie Frazier.

"It's something where you look at a defense for a month," Frazier said in reference to the gap between the final regular season game and the Fiesta Bowl, "and you find a weakness."

Jason Peter said Osborne's halftime speech at the Fiesta Bowl was also motivational.

"Probably the Florida game is the most memorable for me," Peter said. "When we were in there at halftime, Coach Osborne told us just to go out there and basically finish them off and show everybody who the best team in the nation is. He said it with authority and it really got everybody fired up. That's the one thing that I definitely remember."

Jamel Williams said the second national championship solidified Osborne's standing as one of the best coaches of all time.

"It was great for me to be a part of bringing Coach Osborne his first national championship and then the second one," said Williams. "It was special to have them be back-to-back, too. That was the neat thing about it. That makes those teams a great part of Nebraska history and all of college football history. It was really an honor to be a part of that."

Booker was the Defensive Most Valuable Player in the second national title game, a 62-24 thumping of Florida in the Fiesta Bowl on January 2, 1996.

"It felt good to get that award," Booker said, "but it was for the whole team and Coach McBride and Coach [George] Darlington, for having me in the right position and making the right defensive play calls. And the award was for Coach Osborne for believing in me."

The first national title, which came against Miami in the Orange Bowl, was memorable for a lot of reasons.

"Miami talks the talk and they play pretty well, too," offensive guard Brenden Stai, who went on to play for the Pittsburgh Steelers, said the night of the game. "But Coach Osborne isn't about talking smack. This is for him."

Husker rush end Donta Jones, who also went on to play for the Steelers, said it was important to him to get Osborne a national championship for the 1994 season—Jones' senior year.

"We broke the jinx," Jones said.

Every player interviewed about that game said one thing stands out above all others.

"Without question, my most distinctive memory is from halftime of the Orange Bowl game with Miami," Veland said. "We were losing, but he told us we were playing well, just to keep riding it out and we'd wear them down in the fourth quarter. Like a prophet, the words all came true. That confidence that came from Coach during that halftime talk translated right to the players. We went back out there knowing we were going to win."

Playing on the Huskers' strengths and pointing out Miami's weaknesses showed Nebraska where it was headed in the second half of the Orange Bowl—to the top and Osborne's first national championship.

"At the Miami game, he had total confidence in us," Aaron Taylor said. "At halftime, he said, 'Hey look, you guys keep pounding out the yardage against these guys and they're eventually going to fold. They're not in as good of shape as we are.' He could see that as a coach—that they were slowly starting to fall apart. And they did in the fourth quarter. That's how we won our first national championship."

That Osborne had that kind of confidence was impressive enough. Still, the most impressive thing was that the words rang—not just partially true as the second half unfolded—but completely true.

"That was the irony," said offensive tackle Chris Dishman. "He goes up there and describes the second half—and everything he says came true that second half. It was like he could see into the future. He knew there would be penalties. He knew that Miami would do something stupid—and sure enough, they ended up with some dumb penalties. Coach said we would wear them down and that was so evident."

St. Louis Rams linebacker Troy Dumas, a senior during the 1994 title run and a third-round pick of the Kansas City Chiefs in 1995, said the halftime speech at the Orange Bowl is also his most distinctive memory of Osborne, at least when it comes to football.

"There was no question that he had all the confidence in the world, so what he said at halftime did not surprise me," Dumas said. "What surprised me is that everything he said came true, to the letter."

Schlesinger, who had a pair of fourth-quarter touchdowns to help rally the Huskers past Miami, said there were no doubts as to what would transpire in the second half of the 1995 Orange Bowl.

"I knew exactly what was going to happen just by the way he was talking," Schlesinger said. "When he said something, he meant it and knew it was true. When he said that, we all knew it would come true, too."

Center Aaron Graham, a fourth-round pick of the Arizona Cardinals in 1996, said that halftime talk has earned a well-deserved spot in Big Red folklore.

"It didn't really throw me for a loop personally because every time he had something to say, it had a gist to it," Graham said. "That was definitely just a classic speech—that he could be so intuitive and predict what was going to happen."

Zach Wiegert, a 1995 inductee into the Nebraska Football Hall of Fame, had a different take. The Outland Trophy winner said the players admired Osborne so much that they tried to be like him. So Osborne's words were the same Wiegert often used.

"I was thinking what he was thinking," Wiegert said. "You're around him so much; I would always repeat things he said in meetings because the way he put things came out best. So I always mimicked what he said. I started thinking like him, seeing the same things he sees. The things he said at halftime were mostly our game plan going in. We thought we'd wear Miami down."

Tomich said Osborne's confidence and calmness at halftime made the players believe the coach's words as much as ever.

"We were losing at halftime against Miami, and a lot of coaches, when you're losing at halftime, will get restless and loud and say things based on emotion," Tomich said. "But Coach Osborne came into the locker room and said, 'You're playing well and you're playing hard. In the fourth quarter, you guys are going to win.' Everyone was like, 'OK, we'll win.' And that's exactly what happened. And he didn't just say that at halftime; he had been saying the same thing the whole week leading up to the Orange Bowl, that we would win the game in the fourth quarter."

Terry Connealy said the halftime speech at the Orange Bowl wasn't the only time Osborne's halftime vision came true. However, Connealy admits that evening in Miami remains etched in his mind more than two years later.

"I look at it in a lot of the same ways the other guys from that team do," Connealy said. "I remember Coach Osborne telling us, 'They will get mad and they will tire. There will be a personal foul.' We all believed that it was going to happen. We knew Coach Osborne had been in that position before. You always got the feeling, just listening to Coach Osborne, that things would turn out the way he said. After the game was over and we were thinking about it, we thought back to the halftime speech and how almost eerie it was that he hit everything word for word. It was like he was able to see two hours into the future."

Jamel Williams said the much-publicized theory that the strong Huskers would wear teams down in the second half really came to light that night in Miami.

"During the first national championship in Miami, we went into halftime and we were losing," Williams said. "Coach said that eventually Miami would do something to hurt themselves. He said they'd be tired as the second half got going, especially in the fourth quarter. He said, 'Keep playing hard, and we'll get it done.' It was like he knew we would win. We believed Coach Osborne—we always believed what he said. And he was right on with that. In the fourth quarter, we wore them down."

Booker, a reserve in 1994, said he remembers Osborne's half time speech as though it was yesterday.

"For the first national championship, I was still kind of wet behind the ears and just playing on special teams," Booker said. "But when Coach Osborne said that in the locker room, we knew he had to be right. When Coach Osborne talked, we always listened and took it to heart. He knows a lot about the game, so there was never any question that he always knew what he was talking about."

The confidence that was apparent at halftime in Miami was prevalent from the day the Huskers found out they would face Florida in the Fiesta Bowl for a shot at a second straight national championship. Tomich said he had never seen Osborne as confident as he was during the week leading up to the Fiesta Bowl in Tempe, Arizona.

"Before we beat Florida for the second national championship in a row, Coach Osborne was pretty fired up—for him," Tomich said. "He was saying that we would go out and just crush this team. That we would win without any challenge."

While Osborne took the national titles in stride, Grant Wistrom said the titles should put to rest, once and for all, any lingering feeling in the national press about Osborne's ability to win the so-called "big game."

"Coach Osborne can say what he will about the titles," Wistrom said. "I honestly believe him when he says the national championships don't mean much to him. But it really bugs me when people say he can't win the big one or he's not a good enough coach to win the big one and things like that. You know, it wasn't the national title that was so satisfying—actually being labeled 'National Champions.' I think it was perhaps just finally getting the monkey off his back and saying, 'Hey, he is one of the great coaches of all time.' To be a part of that, to help him win that title, means a great deal to me. Coach Osborne isn't the type of guy who is going to dwell on it that much. He's not going to say, 'Hey, this is what I want, this is important to me.' I think I'll probably remember the speeches or something that he said after the national championship game against Florida: 'Enjoy this, but remember, as soon as we get back to Lincoln, we've got to start working for next year.' "

Chris Dishman's second most distinctive memory came after the second national championship win.

"Another time that stuck out was after the Fiesta Bowl," Dishman said. "I remember right after the game, Coach Osborne talked about how we can celebrate for two weeks. But in the third week, we'd start back up preparing for next year. That's just the guy he is. What we did was great. But he was just letting us know that we would have to get back to work and do it all over again."

Ahman Green refers to the "Osborne era" when he talks about his time with the Huskers.

"It felt good because I knew I was part of history in terms of the Osborne era," Green said. "I was one of the guys who contributed to us having the big season, which we did in 1995. I really can't explain how I felt, but I know I felt good that year."

Osborne kept his level head during the national champion rout over Florida. Green hopes that will lead to Osborne getting the credit he is due.

"I know how he felt," Green said. "He probably felt, 'It was just another game that we had to do, and we went out and did it.' He prepared us mentally and physically, and we went out and won the game for him. He gives us most of the credit. But you have to give him some credit, too."

The Huskers lost twice during the season following the second national championship. But in 1996, NU still ended up in the Bowl Alliance. And the Huskers followed that up in 1997 with another national championship.

"You know, I got to contribute to the second national championship and a little bit to that first one, and it was exciting," said All-American guard Aaron Taylor, who also started on the third national championship team in 1997. "It was exciting to see how all the players reacted to it, how the coaches reacted to it and how the fans reacted to it. It was exciting to see that, and I think what's more impressive is that we haven't let down since, and that is awesome."

The players learned to lean on each other and the coaching staff during the tough times. Each of the three runs to the national championship were filled with obstacles. During the first one in 1994, the Huskers survived not only the close Orange Bowl win over Miami, but an early season scare against Wyoming in addition to the health and injury problems at quarterback. The following year, the Big Red dominated on the field, and the only worries—albeit significant ones—were off the field. The final of Osborne's three national titles saw the Huskers survive road scares at Missouri and Colorado.

"As we all know, in a season there's always ups and downs," Turner Gill said. "In those years we won the national championships, there were some ups and down, and times when the players really had to focus on each other, and believe in each other and the coaching staff. We could see how it all fit together—that's what is the most amazing thing here."

# CHAPTER 5

# THE ONE
# THAT GOT AWAY

While going for two—instead of settling for the extra point and a 31-31 tie—which would have guaranteed the Huskers the national championship for the 1983 season, seemed a risky call, All-American offensive lineman and Outland Trophy and Lombardi Award winner Dean Steinkuhler said he would have done the same thing.

"At the time, it was the right decision," Steinkuhler said. "I thought, 'Oh it would've been great to kick the extra point and win the national championship.' But even looking back now, it was the right decision. I would have done that, too. It showed a lot of courage by Coach Osborne. Even to this day, I still feel that was right."

Quarterback Turner Gill threw the two-point conversion pass that was within inches of Jeff Smith and a national championship.

"He's a winner, and he's not scared to take chances," Gill said. "He's consistent in his beliefs and he loves to win. At that moment, the best thing to do was to try to win the football game. That's just a prime example of how competitive he is and how it's just such a hard drive to take every single moment to be the best you can be. That's Coach Osborne."

Gill said the Huskers knew they were within a fingertip of making history.

"We all knew it was an important deal—the first time we had a chance to be national champions and the opportunity to do those things—to achieve it," Gill said. "We knew it was important and we were going to play hard and do the best we could."

Mike McCashland was a defensive back for Nebraska on the 1983 team. Now a successful businessman who owns four fast-food restaurants in Omaha, McCashland remembers how Osborne kept his calm after the two-point conversion attempt failed.

"His expression didn't change—none whatsoever," said McCashland. "He had the same attitude going into every situation. If you play the best you can play, that's all he ever asked for."

Mark Schellen, who played fullback on the 1983 team, said Osborne had decided to go for two points long before the final seconds.

"I played hard; we left everything on the field," said Schellen. "Coach Osborne had a game plan. He even told us during the week that if it came down to it and it was a last-second deal—we'd go for two points. You have to go for it, you really do. You kick the extra point and you get a tie. You are the national champion—but there's no looking back. I had a great opportunity to play football—I appreciate that."

McCashland said that while he believes the Huskers were a much better team than Miami, he did not think NU delivered its best performance that night.

"Defensively, for sure, we didn't play as well as we could have," McCashland said. "That was a home game for Miami and that was probably the loudest crowd I ever witnessed. That place was, by far, the most hostile environment I had ever been in."

Mark Daum was the starting strong side linebacker on the 1983 team.

"That's one thing—he's not wishy-washy, by any means," Daum said. "He makes a decision and sticks with it, even though some people may not agree with it. I look back at all the decisions he made and they were the right ones. He had his own form of confidence. He wasn't arrogant by any means. He just had a sense of confidence about him. A good example was that two-point conversion. To make that decision under those circumstances and all that noise was tough. We all look back at it and that really was the right decision. It still is the right decision."

Middle guard Ken Graeber, now a mechanical engineer in Omaha working in sales at a gas company, said he is still surprised to hear people asking him about the two-point conversion wherever he goes.

"It's kind of funny because people still ask me about that now, 13 years after it happened," Graeber said. "I don't regret it now and I didn't regret it then. Back then, it was not even a question of what we should do."

Daum remembers the final play of the game as if it were yesterday.

"Jeff Smith was the receiver on that conversion pass," Daum said. "It was awfully close. The Miami guy may have tipped it. Otherwise, that would have been Coach Osborne's first national championship."

While many remember only the television replay of the final play of the 1984 Orange Bowl, what sticks out in Daum's mind is what Osborne said in the locker room afterward.

"We came into the locker room and there was a lot of emotion by the players because we left it all out on the field," Daum said. "Coach Osborne came in there and told us he had never been prouder of us. He really brought us out of the doldrums. Of course, he never raised his voice to any of us. He put everything in perspective for us. We went through up and down swings and he kept everything intact. In moments when we were too exuberant, he brought us to the happy medium."

All-American defensive back Bret Clark said none of his teammates considered tying as an option.

"At the time, that's what I would say I would have done—I supported it," Clark said. "I didn't want a tie. They always say tying is like kissing your sister."

Although the perception might have been that the failed conversion pass took away from what Osborne had accomplished, All-American lineman Mark Traynowicz believes just the opposite.

"I think Coach Osborne gained a lot of respect from that play," Traynowicz said. "I've been around the United States quite a bit. The people I talked to, at least before he won the national championships, always mentioned that two-point play and how much respect they have for Coach Osborne for going for two and not the tie. As a player, we never thought twice about it. We didn't want to tie. It never crossed our minds, even though it was a topic of discussion."

As with the other players from that team, McCashland said the choice to go for two was, in fact, the only choice.

"There's never been any regret on that call—no question about it," McCashland said. "I don't see how Coach Osborne could be second-guessed on that call. You don't play to tie. In every game in every sport, there are winners and losers. It just so happened that, by a fingernail, we were the loser in that game."

Harry Grimminger, now the vice principal at Grand Island High School, said no one wanted to tie Miami—not before, during or after the game.

"It's always hard to second-guess a guy who has been as successful as Coach Osborne. I've never second-guessed him," Grimminger said. "Fans and media said we should have just gone for the tie. You tried hard to win, not to tie. It just didn't happen that night."

While Osborne's demeanor didn't change after the game, McCashland remembers the players taking it hard.

"Obviously, everyone was drained of emotion and there were a lot of tears," McCashland said.

While that Husker team is regarded as having the best shot at a national championship of any in the 1980s, McCashland said the teams he played on during his final three years at NU all had legitimate shots at the national title.

"It's something we came so close to," McCashland said. "Those teams back then—there were three teams I played on that really had a chance to win three national championships. In 1982, we got beat by Penn State [27-24 in the third game of the season] and we should've played for the national championship [the Huskers were 12-1]. We would've played Clemson in the Orange Bowl and went in the back door for a national championship. In 1984, in my senior year, we were as good as anyone, but we lost to Syracuse [17-9 in the fourth game of the season] and lost to Oklahoma [17-7] on a fumble in the last game of the regular season."

Dave Rimington, who graduated from Nebraska in 1982, felt his heart sink as he watched the Huskers fall just short of giving Osborne his first national title in the 1984 Orange Bowl. At the same time, he believes the call to go for two was completely justified.

"Coach always made the tough call and we supported it," Rimington said. "Just like in Miami in 1984 going for two in the Orange Bowl, Nebraska didn't go there to tie for a national championship. They went to win a national championship. And winning meant going for two."

Steinkuhler said despite the pandemonium that ripped through the Orange Bowl that night, Osborne's mood was unaffected.

"When we lost that Orange Bowl in 1984, his manner didn't change at all," Steinkuhler said. "He said, 'We didn't win, but we had a chance. Keep your heads up.' I remember how depressed I felt at the time. But I do believe we were No. 1. We could have played Miami again—anywhere—and beat them. I know we were the best team in the nation."

Even when the going got tough, Osborne's demeanor rarely changed, even the slightest bit.

"That's just his personality," Steinkuhler said. "That's the way he was. Things could go to heck real quick, but he was still the same person."

# CHAPTER 6

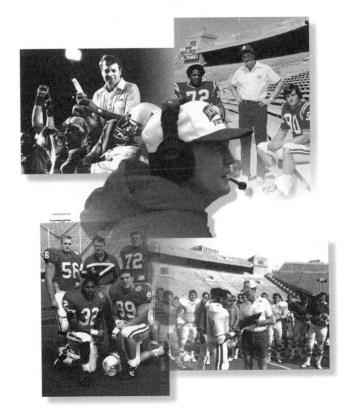

# TOM OSBORNE,
# FATHER FIGURE

*P*layers receive a lot in the form of scholarships to play college football. It is also true that the amount of money is nominal compared to the millions of dollars the players generate for their respective schools. At the same time, Husker players believe they got more than they could have ever asked for when they chose Nebraska.

"I love Coach Osborne just like I love my father and my mother," said Vershan Jackson, a tight end and co-captain on Osborne's final team, which won the national championship.

Chris Dishman, a team captain in 1996, said he had a lot of growing up to do when he arrived in Lincoln.

"He had a big role in my becoming a man," Dishman said. "I had a lot of personal problems when I got there. Now, I'm happily married and have an 18-month-old and another on the way. We really look up to Coach Osborne. He talks about your spiritual life, your mental life and physical life. Those are the three keys. The mental and physical were there for me, but the spiritual wasn't there for me. I've changed on that now, so I can see where Coach Osborne was coming from."

Mark Blazek played for Osborne's 1984 Orange Bowl team. While Osborne's effect on players from single-parent homes is important, Blazek said players coming from stable, traditional families also benefit from Osborne's wisdom.

"You probably hear a lot about how Coach Osborne is a father figure to a lot of the players," Blazek said. "I had a more fortunate upbringing. So, for me, more than anything, he reinforced the work ethic, always behaving properly, that kind of thing. You'd walk in the stadium at 7 a.m. before your first class and Coach Osborne was there. After practice, he's there running laps. So you knew he was putting everything he had into it."

Ironically, Osborne's biggest teaching was often simply reinforcement. Tommie Frazier showed up with a sense of confidence matched only by his magician-like option ability. However, Frazier said Osborne's guidance was as critical to Frazier's success as it was for anyone.

"He taught me to be confident in my abilities," Frazier said. "He was another father figure for me. He cares about you as more than someone who just plays football."

Sheldon Jackson, a tight end on the second and third Osborne national championship teams, agreed with Frazier's assessment.

"He taught me not to be cocky, but don't lack in self-confidence," Jackson said. "Be confident in your abilities and confident in the ability of those around you. If you associate yourself with good people, be confident that they're going to get the job done and do your own job."

Former NU defensive lineman Terry Connealy, a two-time Academic All-American, said he took what he learned from Coach Osborne into his current job as an agribusiness man in western Nebraska.

"I wouldn't trade that for anything in the world," Connealy said. "Those five years in Lincoln were the best five years of my life. What did he teach me? That's tough to tackle with just a sentence. He taught me a lot about the game of football. More importantly, he teaches you how to be a good person and how to carry yourself. What he taught all of us was how to be a good human being."

Mike Minter said the affection the players felt for Osborne actually affected their on-field performance.

"I really hold him in the highest regard that you could hold a human being," Minter said. "Everybody who plays for him views him as a father figure. That was a driving force in our performance, not wanting to let him down."

The look of Osborne's deep blue eyes left a mark on Brenden Stai.

"It's his demeanor that stands out for me," Stai said. "He always had that gleam in his eye that made you know he was someone special. I hold Coach Osborne in the highest regard. I have a lot of respect for the tremendous college football coach he is. More than that, he taught me that life is not about football, but becoming a responsible man. If I was to look back at my time under Coach Osborne, one of the things I would remember is his ability to separate and always know the clear difference between good and bad, or what is right and what is wrong. I'm proud and honored to sit back now and say that I played for Coach Osborne."

The players emulate Osborne's calm and poise, not just on the field, but in the classroom and in their personal lives.

"I think what is really impressive is how he handles himself and how he's taught us to handle adversity," Jason Peter said. "He's a great football coach and everything, but he's just done so much as far as the off-the-field types of things. The way he just doesn't lose his composure and stuff . . . you try to model yourself after somebody like that. He's taught me a lot when it comes to handling yourself as a person."

Grant Wistrom plans to stay in touch with Osborne. And he has little doubt that his former coach will always be there for his players, too.

"What made an impression on me is how much he cares about us," Wistrom said. "I can honestly say if I ever have a problem, if I ever need anything—whether it's next year or 30 years from now— I think I can come to Coach Osborne and he'd do anything within his power to help me out."

Joel Makovicka said the whole process Osborne developed and honed at Nebraska will lead to far more success in life than it ever did on the football field—and that on-field success, keep in mind, was second to none.

"He instilled a great work ethic in being leaders off the field, and he didn't just instill in us how to play great football on the field," Makovicka said. "He kind of prepared us for life off of the field. He tells us not to go through things just for the sake of getting through them. Like in practice, he tells you to go out there and get better in each practice, not just to slide through it, because you will have to work to get better at each particular thing. And that's how it is in life, too."

Matt Davison said the respect between Osborne and the players is unspoken, but at the same time, well-defined.

"Coach Osborne has everyone's attention at all times," Davison said. "We love him like he's our dad. We'd do anything for him, just like he'd do anything for us. It's not just a thing where we have to tell him that, or he has to tell us that—it's just kind of a mutual feeling between the players and him. It's a feeling that can't be described, really."

Ahman Green credits Osborne with keeping the team focused on what it had to do on the field and in the classroom.

"There are a lot of things that he has said," Green said. "He always says to 'Persevere through adversity. You keep your head on straight, no matter what happens in your life, on or off the field. You set your goals right and no matter what is in front of you, trying to break your path, as long as you stay on that path, everything will be all right.' He always told us to keep our heads in any type of situation, whether it was good or bad. He wants us to make sure we have control of the situation and to set goals in life and accomplish them."

Osborne has long been known to stand by his word—without exception. When he recruits players, he tells them he will stand behind them, at the same time demanding they be responsible for their actions on the field, in the classroom and in their personal lives.

"Coach Osborne always stood by his word," Michael Booker said. "He didn't say something unless he meant it. If I could be like anyone, it would be Coach Osborne. Even through adversity, Coach taught us you have to stick to your word and be responsible for yourself."

Jared Tomich, an All-American rush end in 1995 and 1996, said he does not know whether he would have ever graduated from college—much less been afforded the chance—had it not been for Osborne. Tomich had a lot of pride in being part of the back-to-back national championship teams. However, that Tomich graduated before he left Lincoln meant as much as anything. Tomich pulls no punches when he talks about Osborne being the motivating factor in his academic life and leaving Nebraska with a degree before finding the riches of the NFL.

"I will probably tell my children about how important it was to get my degree because of Coach Osborne," Tomich said. "That's all I wanted to do for Coach Osborne. It had nothing to do with football. He gave me so much through the years that I wanted to show him how much I appreciated that by getting my degree. That's why I worked so hard. When I graduated that spring after the national championship, I was so proud for Coach Osborne because I don't know if it would have happened without him and the effect he had on my life."

Former Husker Randall Jobman, who played from 1987-89, said Osborne talked little about football when they first met.

"First and foremost, Coach Osborne wants you to be a Christian and a scholar," Jobman said. "When you've played your last game there, his evaluation of you has nothing to do with whether you go to the pros and make a million dollars. His thing is, 'Did you better yourself?' His sole purpose there was to be there for the kids. He is unlike any other college football coach."

To that end, Osborne always made sure Christianity was there for his players. Whether they chose to pursue it was solely up to the players, Jobman said.

"If you weren't a Christian, he'd asked if you were going to church, especially if you had problems," Jobman said. "Because you learn that your spiritual side does help—I learned that."

Likewise, Osborne continually emphasized the importance of schoolwork.

"He would ask, 'Are you on track to graduate?' before he'd ever talk football," Jobman said. "That was motivation enough for me. I did all right in school and graduated, but I don't think I would have done as well without Coach Osborne."

While wearing the Big Red is motivation for players, Jobman said that wasn't the thing that Osborne used to get his players focused.

"For Coach, it all goes back to who you are, and you play for yourself and your family—what makes you go," Jobman said. "That kind of approach made you more of a solid person, more self-aware and self-motivated. His process showed you that if you want something in life, you have to work for it. If you want to succeed, and you study hard and practice hard, you will succeed. Not everyone sees it at that moment, but five years down the road they all usually see it."

Booker also believes the University of Nebraska football program—which has produced more Academic All-Americans than any other school and regularly leads the conference in graduation percentages—does not get the credit it deserves for pushing its players in the classroom.

"Coach Osborne is about a lot more than winning," Booker said. "He was a father figure to us all. He is the role model for all role models to look up to. That's who I want my kids to be like. He always shot straight with me. A lot of programs aren't like that. He is a straight-up Christian man."

Even when Osborne was hard on players, the players always knew they deserved it. Through Osborne's direction, the players found out the power of being honest and straightforward.

"Coach Osborne is a father figure to all the players off of the field," Jamel Williams said. "You can always count on him. He will always shoot you straight. You might not like what he tells you sometimes, but he's always going to be honest with you. That's just who he is."

Osborne's commitment made the players want to do everything within their power to succeed as well.

"The two things that stand out above anything else are his honesty and work ethic," Aaron Taylor said. "He's up here all the time, and that's exciting to see from a coach, that he is trying to give everything he has in order to better the team. That's a situation where you, as a player, want to do everything you can in order to better the team, too. Because Coach is giving all this effort and you don't want to let him down."

Dealing with the tough times—rather than running around or away from those occasions—helped the Huskers develop the character they needed, not just for the national championship runs, but to make it in the real world.

"You learn a lot about discipline playing for him and the other coaches," Jamel Williams said. "You learn how to deal with adversity. It's never fun to have to do that, but it is something you will have to do in life, whether you like it or not. Coach Osborne taught us to accept that kind of challenge and to learn from it."

John Parrella experienced several periods of self doubt while at Nebraska. However, he leaned on—and continues to lean on—Osborne's words, especially when the going gets tough.

"You can be whatever you want to be if you work hard and have faith in your life," Parrella said. "You can do whatever you want. The fact that I learned that from Coach Osborne and was able to use it in all areas of my life, is probably the biggest impact he had on me."

Whether it was Osborne's rule of not wearing hats inside or simply treating others with respect at every turn, the players were able to realize that the "Golden Rule," by which Osborne lives, is essential for personal and professional success.

"The big thing Coach Osborne teaches us is how to carry ourselves," Tomich said. "He helped us grow up the right way. He made us become men. He taught us so much more than just football. He taught us to always be polite and have manners. He wanted us to handle ourselves in a first-class manner, no matter what we were doing. That didn't necessarily mean wearing suits or anything like that. It just meant how you behaved and how you treated the people you came in contact with. That's really gratifying for me. I still think about that."

Troy Dumas said Osborne affected him personally more than anyone else he's ever met.

"I always remember just the type of man he was, not just that he was one of the best football coaches ever," Dumas said. "He was the greatest. I mean, I don't think I'll ever run across a person who touched me so deeply as a person. Just being around him helped you grow."

While many refer to Osborne as a father figure, Dave Rimington said Osborne was not a brother figure to the players.

"He's a guy who is not super close with the players," Rimington said. "He keeps a distance. At the same time, Coach Osborne has always been there for players who need help. He can't just go around and be everyone's dad. But if you need him, he will take care of you. If you came to him because you made a mistake, he will make sure you don't do it again by having a little talking-to with you."

The love Osborne has for his players is often unspoken. However, it is as visible as the summertime sun from the day the players join NU.

"Coach Osborne is the closest thing you could ever find to a modern-day saint," Tomich said. "He's just so honest and straightforward. He really does love all of his players as though they were his own family."

# CHAPTER 7

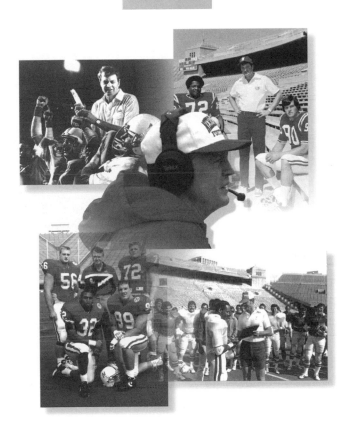

# DOING MORE
# WITH LESS:
# A LEVEL PLAYING
# FIELD?

While Bob Devaney built the program into a powerhouse before Osborne inherited it, Mark Blazek said the fact that Osborne was able to maintain and build upon that success during a time of change in NCAA and conference rules should not go overlooked.

"Coach Osborne turned what was a really good program into what now is the premier program in the country," Blazek said. "I don't think you can look at anyone else over the past 25 years that can compare to Nebraska, whether it's the number of bowls, All-Americans, Academic All-Americans and that kind of thing."

One issue that has not gotten a lot of attention is that Osborne's success came at a time when the playing field was tilted against schools like Nebraska.

"Starting in the 1980s, there has been a constant change in the rules and regulations from the NCAA and the other governing bodies," Blazek said. "Those new rules and regulations have been to the detriment of Nebraska and to the benefit of Florida and California schools. They have limited scholarships, reduced scholarships, reduced visits, cut the position of on-campus recruiter and one year they even limited the food you could get at training tables. Those rules help states with big population bases. Given all these changes, that should have hurt Nebraska and pushed it back to mediocrity, like it did with Iowa and Arkansas. The amazing thing is Coach Osborne and the assistant coaches were able to raise it up a couple of notches. The 10-1 and 9-2 Nebraska teams should have fallen to 6-4 or 7-5. Instead, they became 12-0 and 13-0 and won those national championships."

Despite the changes in the rules, Nebraska actually prospered on the field during a time when everything concerning rules and regulations changes was aligned for a drop-off.

"There has never been a bad season—that's probably the most remarkable thing," Gill said. "You look back at the 25 years and see that he always has won at least nine games every single year. That's unbelievable. You can look back in history and I don't think that you'll ever find anybody in the nation that can match that. There are probably some teams who have more conference championships or teams that have won more national championships—but to say nine wins a year over a 25-year period is just incredible. He has 255 wins in 25 years—an average of 10 wins per season over that time. I don't think that is ever going to happen again, especially with the way scholarship limits are set. And that's exactly what we've done the past four or five years—build more with less, in terms of scholarships and other resources. That's what makes it even more remarkable."

While the scholarships and recruiting rules worked against Nebraska, former offensive lineman Adam Treu said the Husker coaches, led by Osborne, made up the difference through their own extra effort.

"Coach Osborne and his staff work really hard in the off-season," Treu said. "They get almost all of the guys they really recruit hard."

Mike Minter said Osborne always did what he had to do to keep the program moving forward. That meant putting a bigger emphasis on speed at certain times and overhauling the defense on other occasions.

"It all goes back to when he changed his system of defense," Minter said, "because even when the number of scholarships that can be offered went down, there were still good players out there."

The theory of success breeding success worked in Lincoln, Minter said.

"Coach Osborne just had to get the good recruits," Minter said. "With all the success he and Nebraska had, that helped, obviously, in recruiting top players."

# CHAPTER 8

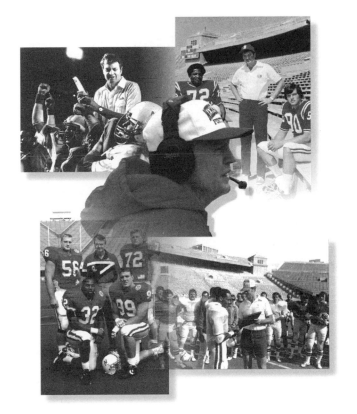

# 'DADGUMMIT!'

*P*layers from the 1986 team remember that year's 35-14 win over Iowa State. Nebraska barely led at halftime.

"He never screamed, yelled, hollered—never used curse words," Denver Broncos defensive end Neil Smith said. "[At Iowa State in 1986], he came in at halftime and said 'Dadgummit, we need to play better.' And that's as close as I ever heard him come to cursing."

Former Husker Broderick Thomas was the sixth pick in the 1989 NFL Draft by Tampa Bay. He played for Detroit and Minnesota before joining Dallas in 1997. Thomas remembers that Iowa State game when, Thomas says, he saw Osborne get "pretty fired up—for Coach Osborne." The Huskers, who would jump from No. 2 to No. 1 in the Top 25 polls, were sluggish against Iowa State in the first half. However, the Huskers rolled in with a strong second half.

"That game, as far as football goes, was the maddest I've ever seen him," Thomas said. "We weren't getting it done against Iowa State. We were getting pushed around by Iowa State. Coach Osborne said, 'Dadgummit, you guys are ranked No. 2 in the nation! Iowa State is not even ranked and they're pushing you guys around. Go out and play some football.' That's the closest thing to a cuss word I ever heard him say. Everyone knows he never actually did curse then or ever. It was shocking to us and the whole coaching staff—everyone in the locker room. He had his Fiesta Bowl watch on from our freshmen year. I remember it that clearly."

Marc Munford looks back on that day at Iowa State with a different kind of memory from the same halftime speech; but it had to do with that same watch to which Thomas referred.

"That was just a brutal day, the wind blowing a million miles an hour in Ames," Munford said. "He said, 'Shoot, we have to hit them on defense!' When he said that, he smacked his hands together and popped his watch off of his wrist. He fumbled around as he put it back on. Then, he said, 'We have to hit them on offense!' And he slapped his hands together, and again, he popped off his watch. It fell down to the floor and he picked it up and put it back on again. This happened, I believe, three or four times. After the third time, it became kind of humorous. No one dared laugh out loud, but there were three or four of us who were holding it in under our breath. I sat there and thought, 'This is it. He's finally going to cuss. He's so mad, he's going to cuss.' He never did, though. He didn't fly off the handle, but that was as mad as I ever saw him."

Mark Blazek was a Husker at that time.

"The halftime of the Iowa State game is definitely what I'll remember," Blazek said. "We had played poorly in the first half. At halftime, we were up 7-6 or 9-6. At halftime, that was the most upset I ever saw him—the most emotion I ever heard from him. He was loud."

And Smith and Thomas weren't the only ones who remember Osborne saying "dadgummit."

"He might have even said 'dadgummit' twice," Blazek said with a smile. "He was certainly red in the face. We hadn't played very well. I can particularly remember a 60-yard running play Iowa State had that I maybe contributed to by missing a tackle up the middle. Brian Davis was 15 yards away from him, but still caught him. Coach Darlington later said, 'You made Brian Davis a lot of money on that play.' Of course, Brian went on to play in the NFL, which is what Coach Darlington was referring to."

The Huskers responded to Osborne's words in the second half.

"We went out," Thomas said, "and handled the business at hand."

Former defensive back Bret Clark remembers a game in Hawaii during the Huskers' 12-1 season in 1982.

"The thing for me was, we were in Hawaii getting beat 16-3 at halftime, I believe," Bret Clark said. "He was pretty mad, that was the maddest I've ever seen him. He said, 'Dadgummit!' It was how he acted, the expression on his face. He had already told us before the game that we were basically down 10 points because of the home-field advantage. His speech at halftime brought it all home to us. We ended up going on a rampage in the second half and beat them 37-16."

All-American Mark Traynowicz remembers a day in 1981 when the Huskers were struggling at home against Auburn. The Huskers rallied after a sluggish first half to win 17-3.

"There was one day when it was raining and we were losing to Auburn at home," Traynowicz said. "We were booed going off the field by our home fans. I think that was the day that Turner Gill took over at quarterback. Anyway, at halftime, Coach Osborne got pretty upset. I think there's even a quote in the locker room hanging up about it to this day. He said, 'The only people who know what we're going through are the players and coaches in this locker room. We will all stick by you.' He said that we have to lean on each other. The fan support was great, but they were booing us."

Mike Minter said the Arizona State game, a 19-0 loss that ended the run of back-to-back undefeated national championship seasons, was the most frustrated he saw Osborne.

"At the Arizona State game, he was pretty mad—then again, we all were," Minter said. "He was just red in the face at halftime. We weren't performing. There was no yelling or screaming on Coach Osborne's part, but I think that was another time where he said 'Dadgummit'—maybe even a few times. Still, what we remember is that he was always calm. All he ever wanted was for us to play our best, regardless of who the opponent was. On that night, we didn't do it."

While 'dadgummit' is the word used to measure the strain Osborne felt at various times, Adam Treu said Osborne was never really that worked up about anything.

"At halftime, he'd occasionally say a 'dadgummit' if we weren't playing up to capabilities," Treu said. "But he really didn't say it that often."

Grant Wistrom, who was named Big 12 Defensive Player of the

Year in 1996 and 1997, has plenty of memories, after playing a key role in each of the national championships. However, Wistrom remembers the come-from-behind 45-38 win over Missouri in overtime in 1997, the most.

"The most memorable moment for me was probably the Missouri game this year [1997]," Wistrom said. "The defense was struggling and Coach Osborne—you know he's kind of the offensive head coach, but he was pretty fired up that game. And he came down and kind of got in the defense's face. He was just like, 'Hey fellas, we gotta get this job done now. So go out there and play some football.' That's one memory that will stick with me. A lot of head coaches won't do that. They don't even coach any positions. They just sit around in their golf cart and drive all over the practice field, just staring at people. Coach Osborne is very hands-on and at that time he felt he needed to get on the defense a little bit—and he did."

For Matt Davison, who made the "miracle" catch on the final play during regulation after Shevin Wiggins had kept the ball alive with his leg, the memory is one of Osborne keeping his calm in the face of ruining what would end up as another undefeated season after the Huskers rallied to win in overtime.

"I won't forget how he kept his composure during the Missouri game, how he got us ready for that last drive," Davison said. "He said, 'All that hard work is going to pay off right here. Let's stick it in the end zone.' "

Aaron Taylor also recalls the Missouri game as a time when Osborne rallied the team.

"He said, 'Fellas, just keep your heads on straight, just keep plugging away and it will turn out for the best.' And it did," Taylor said. "He has a lot of faith in the way things are going to turn out and we have a lot of faith in him. It was good to see that he could predict all that."

Davison added that the rare occasion when Osborne raises his voice means it is really time to buckle down and focus on the task at hand.

"It gets you fired up when he gets fired up, because he doesn't show a lot of emotion," Davison said. "There was one time where we didn't run a play right and he was the most angry he's ever gotten. He said, 'Dadgummit.' That's his favorite word. When he says that, we know we didn't perform up to his expectations. And that makes us work harder."

Still, Davison admits Osborne's displays of emotion were few and far between.

"I think Coach Osborne is just such a humble person," Davison said. "He never lets his emotions overtake him. I think Coach Osborne really has a fire burning inside of him. And I think it's a side of him people really don't see a whole lot. He really wants to win. He gets angry. He gets happy and excited; but he would never do anything to bring attention to himself."

Sheldon Jackson said the players always responded well to Osborne's feedback.

"I've always felt with Coach Osborne running the show, that no matter what was going to happen, we were going to win the game if we did what he told us to do," Jackson said. "He's always been confident in my abilities. I've always felt good when Coach Osborne wanted me in the game to run a specific play. That's something that is going to stick with me until the day that I die—his confidence in me to get the job done. Players don't want to let Coach Osborne down. He puts so much confidence in a specific player to do a certain job on the field—whether it is block that one player, make a catch, get a sack, or whatever—when Coach Osborne wants you in the game and says that he needs you in the game to get something done, you want so badly to get the job done so you won't let him down. The confidence he puts in you—the confidence he has in you—makes a lasting impression.

"He always advocated poise, regardless of the score of the game. Whether we were down by 40 or up by 40, always act as if you're going to get the job done," Jackson continued. "Don't ever go out there and be belligerent, and don't go out there because you're down and start fighting because frustration is starting to set in. He said always act as if you've been here before, because at Nebraska, you have been there before. We've played so many big games here at Nebraska that we are used to all the hype."

While Ahman Green can't point to a particular game, he has little doubt that all of the halftime talks Osborne gave held special meaning.

"His halftime talks were always keen and pointed," Green said. "He always told us, 'We've gotta keep going, keep things going, keep things rolling the way we did in the first half and don't let this slip up here and there.' I would say the halftime talks were the best things."

All players remember Senior Day when each NU senior is introduced before the game. Osborne talks about how much it means to him as he offers a handshake to each player. However, in most cases, that handshake turns to a hug as the player feels a handshake just isn't representative enough of what their time with Osborne meant to them.

"Senior Day at Memorial Stadium was the most emotional day for me," Michael Booker said. "I came out of the tunnel and gave Coach Osborne a hug. I have a picture of it in my photo album. You can tell it's not a fake hug or a courtesy hug. It was a passionate embrace because that man was like a father to me. It was a hug of love for all Coach Osborne did for me."

Jared Tomich remembers the meeting Osborne had with the seniors during Tomich's senior season.

"There weren't many dry eyes in the room," Tomich said. "You always felt cared for at Nebraska. But when he came up to each of us and told us how much he appreciated our efforts, it was really touching. Because, really, it should have been us thanking him because he helped a lot of us change our lives."

Terry Connealy, who graduated with a degree in agribusiness after earning All-Conference honors as a defensive lineman, ranches in the western Nebraska town of Hyannis and is a member of the radio crew that does Nebraska football games.

"I think for everyone who plays down there and has the Senior Day for their last home game, it's a very touching moment,"

Bob Devaney and his successor, Tom Osborne share the
football, and a smile, at Memorial Stadium.

A youthful looking Tom Osborne stands on the sideline during a game in 1973.

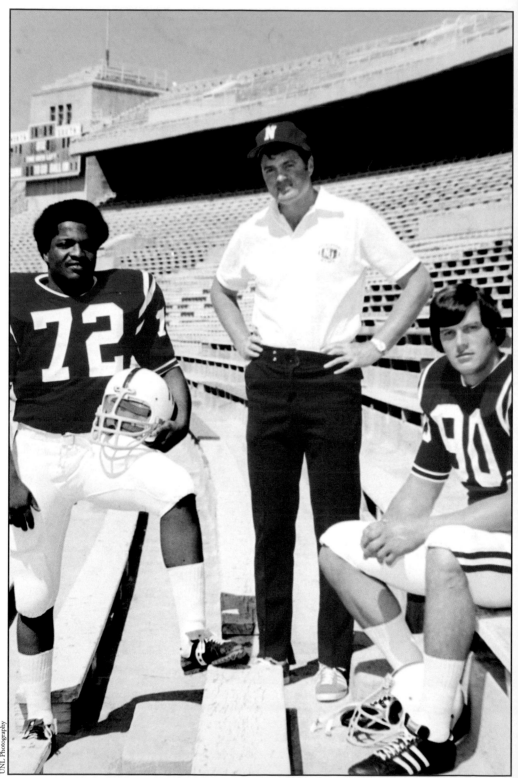

Tom Osborne with his first football Captains, Daryl White (72)
and John Dutton (90) in 1973.

Tom Osborne stands with his 1976 football Captains,
Clete Pillen (61) and Vince Ferragamo (15).

Tom Osborne presents former defensive back Russell Gary with the Lifter of the Year Award in 1980.

Tom Osborne receives a ride off the field following an Orange Bowl victory over Louisiana State in 1983.

Coach Osborne's lone Heisman Trophy winner, Mike Rozier, picks up yardage
during the 1983 season in a game against UCLA.

Coach Osborne and receivers coach Ron Brown
discuss play selection with All-American quarterback Tommie Frazier.

Coach Osborne and former backup quarterback Brook Berringer surrounded by many of their awards from the back-to-back national championships. Berringer died in a plane crash on April 18, 1996. The Husker team established an award in his honor called the "Brook Berringer Citizenship Team."

Coach Osborne's 1994 national championship co-captains: Rob Zatechka (56),
Zach Wiegert (72), Ed Stewart (32) and Terry Connealy (99).

Tom Osborne stands on a platform at Memorial Stadium during the ring
ceremony honoring the 1994 National Championship team.

The dominating defensive line for the Blackshirts during the 1996 season:
Grant Wistrom (98), Jeff Ogard (97), Jason Peter (55) and Jared Tomich (93).

Quarterback Scott Frost talks with Coach Osborne during the Huskers'
victory over Kansas during the 1996 season.

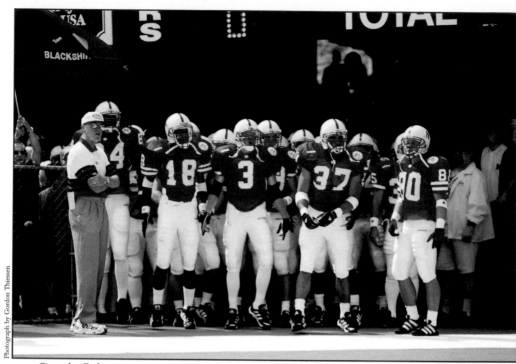

Coach Osborne prepares to take the field with his final Husker football team.

After 250 victories, Coach Osborne takes a moment to talk about his career.

University of Nebraska athletic director Bill Byrne (left) stands on the field at Memorial Stadium as Coach Osborne is honored for his 250th career win.

As part of the celebration of Coach Osborne's 250th career win a display of fireworks takes place over Memorial Stadium.

Coach Osborne watches his team from the sideline during his final season.

This was one of Grant Wistrom's most memorable moments as Coach Osborne
fires up the defense during the 1998 FedEx Orange Bowl game.

Tom Osborne gets his thoughts together in December of 1997 as he
announces he will retire as Nebraska's coach.

Coach Osborne stands with then assistant
head coach Frank Solich on the field before a game.

Connealy said. "It's the end of what you've been doing for the last four or five years. It didn't hit me real hard until a few days after the game when we were practicing on the field at Memorial Stadium. I realized I would never play another game for Coach Osborne at Memorial Stadium."

Booker said Osborne is known for caring for all of his players. He said people would see that more than ever if they were able to witness the last meeting Osborne had with the seniors each year.

"Coach Osborne called the seniors to a meeting and I will never forget it," Booker said. "The thing that struck me was that he knew everything about every player—his major, his interests, his family, everything. He went up to one of the seniors who didn't play much and talked about everything in that guy's life. It was like, 'Wow, how can he know all that about that many players?' "

The players who were on the team that had a shot at the national title in 1983 remember more than just the Orange Bowl. Indeed, a little-known story about fishing showed Osborne's competitive nature.

"I think there had been something arranged for players to attend a function," Harry Grimminger said. "We decided to fish behind the motel. We had a school of fish come through and caught several of them. Coach Osborne was impressed."

"The only time we ever fished together was at the Orange Bowl in 1982," Ken Graeber said. "There were a few of us—Harry Grimminger, Mark Traynowicz and I—who didn't want to go to a few of the optional functions. Well, there was this stream behind the motel we were staying at, where the Miami River met Miami Bay. Harry, Mark and I walked to a store and bought some fishing poles and a bag of lures. Coach Osborne asked what I had in the bag, and it was just a big sack of lures. He kind of snickered at it, because he was such a fisherman. Harry, Mark, and I went down and caught some nice snook—three of them—between 10 and 15 pounds. I wondered what I should do with them. They talked me into showing them to Coach Osborne. I showed them to Coach. So Coach Osborne went and bought a fishing rod. We only had a couple of lures. Coach Osborne brought his wife, Nancy, down to fish with him and they joined us. I think he got snagged on some rocks. It was kind of funny, because he didn't say anything. But there was a competitive nature about him. I could tell he was disgusted when he got snagged and had to hang it up because he had no more lures."

"Coach Osborne fancies himself quite a fisherman—and he is," Grimminger said. "But the night he fished with us in Miami, he just had no luck."

Another memory for former players is that Osborne made the team keep its head and composure all the time, even in practice. Ken Graeber said Osborne made it clear from the first day of practice that cussing would not be tolerated and there was a penalty for doing it.

"He practices what he preaches in terms of solid values," Graeber said. "He makes you run laps for swearing in the huddle at practice. That's something that shows you the discipline and respect he commands, because guys 18 to 23 years old swear too much sometimes. But he put an end to that for each player, after a few laps."

Marc Munford never had to run steps for swearing. But his endurance was built on missed assignments. Munford admits to dropping a few pounds of sweat for that.

"I never had to run laps for swearing, but I used to run a lot of stadium steps for missing guard calls," Munford said. "In the 5-2 defense, you had to make a read. If you didn't, that messed up the defense. I had my fair share."

# CHAPTER 9

# REFLECTIONS FROM OSBORNE'S FINAL TEAM

$W$hile the media often second-guessed Osborne, his players always had faith in their coach's decisions.

"It seems like Coach Osborne does everything right," Jason Peter said. "You know everything he stands for is right—the way he handles himself, the way he handles adversity."

Osborne never was one to say anything that really caught anyone off guard. But that in itself was what appealed to his players, according to quarterback Scott Frost.

"Coach Osborne never says anything really earthshaking," Frost said. "I think the thing that leaves an impression on you is his consistency, his state of mind and that he's able to be steadfast and stay strong through everything. I think that if we take that away from playing here, then that's the most important thing."

Frost said he's even given in to the idea that games are won with Osborne's stable, consistent and predictable ground attack, not the high-flying mentality associated with throwing the ball 50 times a game.

"Being around Coach Osborne, you see how it's supposed to be done, how everything is supposed to be done," Frost said. "I'm a quarterback and I like to throw the ball and he's even got me convinced that running the ball is the way to win games. So a lot of things he does rub off on you and there's no part that isn't good."

Sheldon Jackson recalls a day from the fall of 1997 when he and Osborne spoke.

"There was one thing recently that happened," Jackson said. "We were working out one day together in the corner of the weightroom. He said, 'Sheldon, you're going to be the president of some company someday.' I was thinking about it and I continued lifting. Then I asked him, 'What do you mean, exactly?' He said. 'I just see it for some reason. You're going to be the president of a company sometime soon after college. And when that's all said and done, you're going to come back and buy one of these press boxes, and you're going to invite me up there to watch the games with you.' That kind of stuck with me."

Osborne's "process" of developing boys into men left quite a mark on Grant Wistrom.

"He's a great man, one who I am honored to have known," Wistrom said. "Every day, I thank God for having me come here to play football for such a great person. I feel lucky that I got to spend four years with him. I learned to be a good person and to treat people fairly. It's not necessarily always important where you end up. It's how you get there and just maintaining dignity at all times."

Many players said they were able to harness their temper playing under the calm Osborne.

"He's one of the big reasons why I came to Nebraska," Jason Peter said. "He's got such composure about him and that's the main reason why I chose to come to Nebraska. It's a privilege to play for him. But you learn things like that, like how he handles the adversity and certain pressures. It's just amazing."

Osborne's selflessness was demonstrated to Peter numerous times. However, the caring, nurturing side of Osborne was never more apparent than it was when Peter's younger brother, Damian, broke his neck while playing for Notre Dame.

"After Damian broke his neck, Notre Dame kind of just pushed him away to the side," Peter said. "Coach Osborne had no obligation to Damian or anything. Coach Osborne took him in, told him to come out here and they would do all the medical research on his neck and see if there was an opportunity for Damian to play again. Coach didn't have to do that. Now, Damian's out here and he's going to school. He can't play anymore. But for Coach Osborne, there was no need for him to do that. But that's just the type of person that he is."

Joel Makovicka said that with time, he will be able to reflect on other memories. But as Christmas 1997 approached, he could not get the day Osborne announced he was retiring out of his mind.

"The biggest thing I'm going to remember is his retirement and when he came in and told us that," Makovicka said. "It was kind of a weird experience."

The players know they will be able to share their memories of Coach Osborne with their children someday.

"I will tell my children that I played for the best coach that ever coached college football, or ever coached football," Aaron Taylor said. "I'll tell them that I played for a man who stood for a lot of things and to possibly try to grow up like him. It's a situation where I know I played for the best man ever."

Ahman Green, an All-Conference running back in 1997, said he might not know the words he will pass on to his children about Coach Osborne, but he does know that time will come.

"I don't know what I will say to my kids yet," Green said. "But I know I probably will have a long talk for them about Coach Osborne when that time comes around."

Joel Makovicka said Osborne's biggest influence may well be on how the players take what they learned from him and apply it, eventually, to fatherhood.

"I'll tell my kids how Coach Osborne always taught his players to be better people, not just better football players," Makovicka said. "I'll tell my kids about him. No one is going to forget Coach Osborne."

There is almost no doubt that Osborne has stepped out of coaching for good. But Jason Peter is holding out hope that Osborne will one day return to influence Peter's children the way he has Peter himself.

"Hopefully, he'll be back in coaching by then and my kids can come play for him," Peter said. "I'll be able to tell them what a great guy he was and how honored I was to have the chance to play for him—and that it really was a privilege. There'll be a lot of stories I'll be able to tell about Coach Osborne."

Although he got to play only one year for Osborne, Matt Davison said he has enough memories of Osborne to last a lifetime.

"I'm going to tell my kids that it was an honor to play for this man, this legend," Davison said. "He's going to affect me for the rest of my life. Just being with him this year . . . he's going to be around for the rest of the years that I'm here, even though he won't be the head coach. He helped develop me as a person. And I'm going to pass some of the things that I learned from him down to my children.

"He's taught me how to be a man and the difference between right and wrong, not that I didn't know that when I got here," Davison said. "He taught us to do the right thing in every situation, on the football field and off the football field. He teaches you how to be a man and that football is a small part of life, and that in life as a whole, football is down on the totem pole."

# CHAPTER 10

# REFLECTIONS
# FROM FORMER
# HUSKERS

$W$hile one might expect that the on-field success made for good memories, most former Huskers point to particular times with Osborne as a highlight. Through Osborne's deep faith, many found their own spirituality.

"I don't know if there's one particular thing I will take with me from my time with Coach Osborne. There's just so much that I learned," Tony Veland said. "I'll take a lot of things with me for the rest of my life. His faith in God was so impressive. I will one day tell my children that I played for the best coach in the history of college football—probably the best coach in any sport at any level."

Turner Gill calls the process the most rewarding part of his continuing involvement with Osborne and the NU program.

"I have definitely learned from Coach Osborne that the most exciting thing is just seeing how the players have achieved what they wanted," Gill said. "It's very, very gratifying. I am just glad to be a part of that process, to see how you can achieve these things and see how your players thrive together."

Tom Rathman, an assistant coach for the San Francisco 49ers, said Osborne followed Bob Devaney's model and built on it, taking the program to new heights.

"More than anything, what stands out for me is his honesty," Rathman, a native of Grand Island, said. "He is a very calm and honest individual. He's up there with Bob Devaney, a legend. To be from Nebraska, I was able to see how Coach Osborne just kind of took control of Nebraska's program after Bob retired. He didn't let it slip a bit and he built on it."

Bret Clark works at the Nebraska state penitentiary in the maintenance department. He said while his job today seems different from playing for Osborne, the ingredients for success remain the same.

"For me, it was to be able to concentrate on the problem at hand, just like I do now, being prepared," Clark said. "That's what Coach Osborne always showed me."

Rathman said Osborne had everyone's attention without demanding it. In other words, Osborne commanded respect.

"More than anything, you take with you the discipline you must have playing there," Rathman said. "He didn't yell or anything. But when he was on the field, he was always in total control. You have to have that as a coach."

Mark Traynowicz saw the same dichotomy about which Rathman spoke.

"He's just a great person," Traynowicz said. "He was someone who was respected. He never gave emotional speeches, yet you always wanted to play hard for him. It's hard to explain."

Ken Graeber has a similar recollection.

"The thing I admired is he was able to coach, to be completely in command without ruling with an iron fist," Graeber said. "He didn't scream, yell or physically push you around. But there was no doubt who was absolutely in control."

Chris Dishman said Osborne's calm hid a competitiveness that only those within the program knew.

"People know he doesn't show much emotion, but he's such a competitor," Dishman said. "You can't see it from the stands, but he wanted to bust a big play every time. If we did badly, sure he was upset; he just didn't show it. But he had such a fire in him. His competitiveness is what I will always remember."

Aaron Graham was the center for the back-to-back national championship teams. After graduating following the 1996 Fiesta Bowl, Graham was drafted by the Arizona Cardinals.

"The thing that I appreciated is you hear people who talk the talk, but you wonder if they walk the walk," Graham said. "Coach Osborne walks the walk. That's impressive. You know how you always hear that he's on the same keel? Well, that's just so true. No one can say, 'Well, there was this time in a meeting when he just lost it.' Or, 'There was this game and he just got so mad and started yelling.' No one ever saw that from Coach Osborne. It was just never like that. He always kept things in perspective."

John Parrella, who was drafted by the Buffalo Bills after playing in the Huskers' 18-16 loss to Florida State in the 1994 Orange Bowl in a game for the national championship, is now with the San Diego Chargers. Ironically, Parrella's college career started with the same sort of change of scenery.

"I was going to Colorado. I had signed at Colorado," Parrella said. "Before I even went to Boulder, it didn't work out for me there. So I ended up going to Nebraska before I attended Colorado. Back when I had announced I was going to CU, Nebraska wrote me a letter, congratulating me and saying if, for whatever reason, things ever changed, that I could still call on Nebraska. So when things went bad for me at CU, that's the first thing I thought of—Nebraska. They were happy to have me. That's the biggest blessing in disguise I had my whole life."

The national championships and the chance to play in the NFL are just a few of the things for which Zach Wiegert credits Osborne.

"I owe everything I have, everything I've done to Coach Osborne and Nebraska," Wiegert said.

Wiegert, who graduated from Fremont Bergan High School, said he seized on Osborne's words to become the best player he could be, which resulted in a score of All-American honors before being picked in the second round of the 1995 NFL Draft by the St. Louis Rams.

"Coach Osborne tells most of the kids that if you can work your way up, in a year or two you make a contribution," Wiegert said. "That was my intention. But after my first or second year, I thought I could do better."

Like the others in the NFL, Wiegert misses the emotional highs from fall Saturdays in Lincoln.

"I was depressed during the week," Wiegert said. "I really looked forward to game days. Coach Osborne would tell you that I wasn't Mr. Practice. The games were my thing. I loved running out on that field."

The way Osborne handled himself made the players want to act the same way. It meant making the right choice when the wrong one might have been easier or more convenient.

"I strived to be the best role model I could be off the field for Coach Osborne," Michael Booker said, "especially when we had those incidents, like the one with Lawrence Phillips [a football player who found trouble off the field]."

Steve Forch, who works for a professional business service company, said he took the work ethic he learned under Osborne and applied it to the business world.

"Going through the process of playing at Nebraska and having to work for everything really helped me," Forch said. "I was a five-year guy and I had to really push myself to get to the top of the starting lineup. I went from being a bit player to being All-Big 8 and being drafted into the NFL. I was known to have a little fun. Let's put it this way, I wasn't a choirboy. But he knew what kind of player he wanted, someone who would stick around and had skills that he could develop. It was just a matter of recognizing where the right talent is."

Harry Grimminger, a native Nebraskan, said no one treasures playing for Osborne more than home-state players.

"The most valuable lesson that he teaches is the notion of character," Grimminger said. "He has a great deal of integrity. He's very honest with people. His work ethic, of course, is beyond reproach. Just the character he has and how he communicates that to his players is a memory I'll always have. The players who participate in the Nebraska program are proud to have done so, especially the players who hail from the state. Coach Osborne is the kind of guy who leaves a lasting memory."

While the nation sees Nebraska as only a red letter on a white helmet, John Parrella said the program runs a lot deeper, both on and off the field.

"A lot of people think you go there for five years, you play great football and that's all there is to it," Parrella said. "But it really is a big growth period for kids that age. Things weren't always the best for me. I had to learn to be a man. Coach Osborne was and is always there for me. Quite a few times, they could have said, 'We don't need you.' That never happened."

The occasions did come up when the players would not be very happy practicing at certain times, whether they were tired or if the weather wasn't accommodating. Still, they had enough belief in Osborne and the coaching staff to know that everything was done for a reason.

"Sometimes we were practicing outside when we, as players, thought we should be inside," Booker said. "But that was the only time we ever complained. And there was a reason we were outside, we just couldn't see it at the time. But no one ever said a bad word about Coach Osborne."

Likewise, no former Husker player interviewed for this book could remember Osborne ever uttering a bad word about anything or anyone.

Toby Wright said he still pictures Osborne walking out to practice or to film study sessions.

"I have never seen someone walk with such a strong aura about them," Wright said. "He's not a big man and his walk is sort of awkward, with kind of a limp. But you see the strength and dignity just in his walk."

While other coaches, especially in the now defunct Big 8, liked to play up the Nebraska game, Osborne never did recognize rivalries.

"That's what I liked about him, he never got blown up about anything," Dishman said. "He'd take every game serious. Someone might play up rivalries, but not Coach Osborne. A lot of coaches say that one-game-at-a-time cliche´. But Coach Osborne lived that philosophy. He was a coach who said, 'We're the team to beat. We're the best in the nation.' He made us feel that way. That confidence was just another positive. He instilled that in our minds."

All former players know they played for someone who was about far more than football, according to Terry Connealy.

"You look at a lot of people in Coach Osborne's position and I don't think any stack up to him as far as his honesty, integrity and his work ethic," Connealy said. "That rubbed off on everyone who played for him. I hold him in the highest regard. The people who played for him end up being good, honest people. They saw that example from Coach Osborne."

Almost all former players try to find their way back to Lincoln. They treasure even the shortest interaction with Osborne. And the memories they have from Lincoln are rarely surpassed, even in the NFL.

"I came back to Lincoln before we [the Redskins] played the New York Giants the first time this year," Jamel Williams said. "Coach Osborne said, 'Good luck. I'm proud of you.' Retiring will be good for him because now he can enjoy everything he has accomplished. He can relax and take it easy, just kind of sit back and spend time with his family or go fishing. He's earned it."

Former players say that Osborne is as genuine as he appears. They also know the confidence he has in himself, his players and his coaching staff often goes unnoticed outside of Nebraska.

"Coach Osborne has got that quiet confidence," Dave Rimington said. "He won't blow his own horn, but he has confidence. He underplays it. But he has to have that kind of confidence to be a success. I see that public perception that a lot of people, especially out of the state, have—that 'Oh shucks' kind of image. But I know he's not always that way because I've heard him in the locker room."

Mike McCashland played defensive back for Nebraska's 1983 Orange Bowl team. A successful businessman in Omaha now, McCashland took what he learned from Osborne and applied it to the business world.

"Coach Osborne's process was about always setting goals and working within a structure," McCashland said. "The structure he set is one that will never be duplicated. Those of us who played for him took that off the field, too. Because to succeed in business, you have to go in with discipline. It's not always fun, but you have to have the right attitude day in and day out."

While the national titles ensured Osborne's legacy, Mark Blazek said the sheer volume of wins made sure Osborne's accomplishments would not go overlooked.

"I don't think it would've made a difference to Coach Osborne, personally, if he had not won the national championships," Blazek said. "It certainly plants him squarely atop the greatest coaches in college football history. You can't win that many games for that long and go unnoticed. But had he not won the national championships, the national press might have overlooked him a little more."

And, Blazek said, it all comes back to the "process."

"He really does mean it when he talks about the process and hard work being the important things, much more so than all the victories," Blazek said. "The process and working toward the goal were what I remember. I was like that before I went to Nebraska, so Coach Osborne just reinforced that. It's all about working toward a goal, even though it is nice to win the big games and be the champion. But it is all about the process. If you apply the process and work ethic to whatever you are doing, you will be the best at it. That's what Coach Osborne has done at Nebraska."

The unspoken confidence that exudes from Osborne stays that way, keeping in line with Osborne's public persona of being rather reserved.

"The thing about Coach Osborne is stability and the quiet integrity," Rimington said. "He's a man who doesn't talk just for the sake of talking. I've been around coaches who talk for no reason. They just make things up as they go. Coach Osborne likes the stable environment around him."

Mark Schellen, a fullback for the Huskers in 1982-83, called Osborne a true "gentleman."

"I remember Coach Osborne as a decent gentleman who worked hard to prepare his team," Schellen said. "He cared a lot more about the players off the field than he did on the field. He expected you to be good on the field. But he kept you in line off the field."

Osborne's ability to see the big picture—keeping together a

coaching staff with 150-plus combined years of experience and helping NU stay among the leaders in facilities—should not be overlooked. In an era unsurpassed for parity in college football, Osborne made sure all bases were covered.

"He's kept his assistant coaches because he treats them well and recognizes that they're valuable," Rimington said. "That is a draw for recruits to the University of Nebraska. And it was always important to Coach Osborne to have top-notch facilities. He knows he is competing with schools in Florida that have a great climate. So if you are in the Midwest and you have the kind of winter that Lincoln is known for, then you'd better have good facilities. Most recruits must be in awe of the weight room and everything at Nebraska. Coach Osborne and the people he's surrounded himself with are smart enough to know they have to meet—and exceed—those expectations."

Rimington, who works in New York, said he still treasures his trips back to Lincoln, especially when he is able to see Osborne.

"We do a fundraiser called Husker Preview," Rimington said. "Coach Osborne asked me how it was going. Coach Osborne always asks about my family and my little brother. To give you some context here, my 'little' brother weighed something like 300 pounds when he was 15 years old. So Coach Osborne would ask, 'How big is your brother now?' He's always asked about my mother and how she was doing. Even small talk with Coach Osborne is always a pleasure. He's one in a million, and there might not even be that many people like that."

While Osborne took shots from the national media over the years, Rimington said he was glad to see the coverage be almost entirely positive when Osborne resigned. While the media's coverage was different in approach, Tom Osborne, the man, did not change.

"He's just such a great guy and is so honorable," Rimington said. "Everybody who knew him was aware of that all along. Now that he's stepped down, everyone is saying that they saw that side all along."

Like many former Huskers who made it to the NFL, Toby Wright cites his time in Lincoln as among the most important years of his life.

"Being able to play for Coach Osborne and play at Nebraska was the best thing that ever happened to me," Wright said. "I was at a point in my life after junior college where I could have gone either way in life. I was pretty mature, but I was still looking to find myself. I accomplished all that in Lincoln."

Cory Schlesinger, who hails from Duncan and graduated from Columbus High School, said fans and players in the NFL asked about the Nebraska mystique and what it was like to play for Osborne.

"People asked me that a lot," Schlesinger said. "You could go on and on about Coach Osborne. But what I tell people is just that Coach Osborne is a great role model."

Donta Jones, a rush end on Osborne's first national championship team in 1994, said Osborne is still affecting his life, even though Jones is a linebacker with the Pittsburgh Steelers.

"He taught me to be self-motivated and work hard, just to be a good role model," Jones said. "All of the players I know . . . we just loved playing there. It really motivated us, knowing the type of person Coach Osborne is. He was not just a coach. He was a father figure as well. He looked out for your best interest. We felt like we owed him a national championship."

Steinkuhler was an All-American at Nebraska. But his affection for Osborne did not start until he was well into the program at Nebraska.

"Probably, at the time, Coach Osborne was not as big of a factor as you'd think as to why I picked Nebraska," Steinkuhler said. "I just wanted to play for Nebraska. I was a little shellshocked at how good all the players were."

However, after being around Osborne the first few times, Steinkuhler saw why all the players held Osborne in such high regard.

"Looking back, when Coach Osborne said something, I didn't

really think he was saying it to me," Steinkuhler said. "As you look back, everything he said was true and it applied to everyone to varying degrees."

Another comment from Osborne stuck with Steinkuhler, who went on to play eight years for the Houston Oilers.

"One other thing that Coach always talked about was that the program was successful," Steinkuhler said. "He said, 'You won't remember the ones you won; you'll remember the ones you lost.' He said that to keep you motivated and so you didn't get used to losing. You win so many games while you are there, it really is unbelievable."

While many individual players went on to have successful careers in the NFL, Steinkuhler said the Huskers' effort was a team effort from start to finish.

"It makes me very proud to have played for Coach Osborne," Steinkuhler said. "You have to remember, we had [Mike] Rozier, [Turner] Gill and Irving Fryar, just to name a few. I had good guys around me."

John Parrella said Osborne's demeanor, whether it is winning big or the occasional loss, never changed much.

"The thing I really remember about Coach Osborne," Parrella said, "is that it didn't matter if we beat Colorado 52-7 or that loss to Iowa State (19-12 in 1992), Coach's emotions never changed. Even when we lost, he always said, 'If you play well, you will have a chance to win. If you don't, you can expect to lose.' Whether the situation was good or bad, his emotions never changed. He just never seemed to have a bad day. That gave you a feeling of stability and always believing in the program."

Like many other players, Marc Munford called Osborne one of the most influential people in his life.

"I look at Coach Osborne as almost a flawless kind of person," Munford said. "I never tried to model myself after him, even though I do respect what he's done. You have to blaze your own trail, which he encouraged us to do. You treat people the way you want to be treated. That's kind of common-sense stuff, but young men have to be reminded of that as they grow up. We all make mistakes. What Coach Osborne asked is that we learn and grow from them."

Turner Gill shares that same view.

"Really, I look back at my life and I know he was very influential," Gill said "The person that I am today is definitely an example of Coach Osborne because I really believe in the things he does and the way he talks about it. What Coach Osborne really got going for me is the spiritual part of things. I remember him in meetings. At certain times, he would talk about a Scripture in the Bible and share some of those things with us. Really, Coach Osborne is the person who led me to Christ, just by example, the way he did things. The spiritual thing is something that really, really stands out in my mind. I had him in my wedding as a groomsman."

Adam Treu said he hopes Osborne knows how deeply he affected Treu and the other players.

"He did a lot for me and for thousands of other guys," Treu said. "A lot of the non-Nebraska raised players are imported from a long way from Lincoln. Coach Osborne and the assistant coaches do all they can to help them make it there."

Treu said his Nebraska background under Osborne was often the topic of conversations during his rookie year in the NFL in 1997 for the Oakland Raiders.

"Lots of players asked me, 'What was it like to play for Coach Osborne at Nebraska?' " Treu said. "I just tell him that we all have so much respect for the coach, it is amazing. I tell everyone how fortunate I was to play for Coach Osborne and the other coaches. I tell [them that] Coach Osborne was great. He is a great man who doesn't cuss or swear."

John Parrella said Osborne dealt with problems fairly, but made sure players knew there would be a price to pay if they broke the rules.

"I always felt like he was our dad," Parrella said, "but if you made a mistake, he was on you. He didn't come across as he would stop liking you or loving you. All he wanted you to know is that what you did was wrong. He would say, 'This is how to correct it. I will support you and help you, but you have to address it yourself, too.' I've heard of a lot of coaches at other schools who get in your face and really scream at you."

Former Husker Randall Jobman is looking forward to telling his young children about the time he spent under Coach Osborne in Lincoln.

"Coach Osborne is a legend," Jobman said. "He'll go down in the record books and be in the Hall of Fame one day. I was fortunate to be able to play in that era, take away some things he taught me and what he stood for. I have two children now. Twenty years from now, they'll probably read this and that about Coach Osborne. But I'm lucky. I'll be able to tell them everything personally."

Mark Traynowicz said he does not get back to Husker games very often. But when he and his former teammates get a group together to go, Traynowicz said the highlight is seeing Osborne again.

"It was interesting because we all went back to a game—Mark Daum, Ken Graeber, Rob Stuckey, Harry Grimminger," Traynowicz said. "We saw Coach Osborne down by the locker room. It was just like we were still his players. He remembered all of our names. He asked Ken Graeber about fishing. It is just amazing that thousands of kids have played for him and he remembers all of them personally."

That also means a lot to Graeber.

"He's amazingly personable to all of us," Graeber said. "I've been down to games on two or three occasions. He always stopped what he was doing and made a point to come over and personally visit with you and show genuine interest. He's seen thousands of kids go through, yet he seems to remember stuff about all of us."

# CHAPTER 11

# OSBORNE
## AT THE IMPROV?

*D*uring the final three or four years of his tenure as head coach, Tom Osborne could often be seen catching the media off-guard with one of his one-liners. It was an intellectual kind of humor, analytical and intelligent rather than sarcastic and spiteful.

Osborne's sense of humor is, much like the coach himself, very contained and subtle.

"Coach has got this very dry sense of humor," Jason Peter said. "But he really is one of the funniest guys I know. When the cameras are shut off and everything, he's a very relaxed guy. Especially this year (1997), we've had a lot of fun together and we're always joking around with each other. He's just a lot of fun to be around and to talk to."

"Dry" is the word most often used to describe Osborne's sense of humor.

"He doesn't come off as a humorous person, but he's always joking around with the players and coaches," Turner Gill said. "He comes up with all sorts of jokes and stories that have come along during his time and are part of him. I can't say that it's brought out into the public—which I think is fine, because he's still a private person. He's a person with a little bit more of a dry humor."

"He has an extremely dry sense of humor," Sheldon Jackson said. "I have some of that in me. But I think Coach Osborne might have the dry kind of humor. He's not going to go out there and crack jokes on just anybody. I think you have to pay attention to what he's saying to catch his jokes. But he's not as laid back as people would like to think he is."

Osborne's sense of humor is as unique as the coach himself.

"He makes jokes every once in a while to the media," Matt Davison said. "But during meetings and stuff like that, he'll come up with one every once in a while. It's a sense of humor that's a one-of-a-kind thing, just like Coach Osborne is. When he cracks a joke or something, it really opens things up and lets us all lay loose for a second before we get back to work."

Osborne's sense of humor provided more insight into the man who few in the public, especially outside of Nebraska, ever knew.

"He has a wit and a lot of humor in him that a lot of people don't see, and just we players see it," Aaron Taylor said. "That's how we feel at ease with him. I don't have a particular story, just seeing him crack a joke and seeing that smile on his face—it gives you a feeling that I will never forget. He talks about Joel Makovicka being short and he always had that little smile or smirk on his face. You just never forget that. You can go up to him in the middle of practice and throw a couple of jokes at him and he'll joke back at you. A lot of people don't see that side of Coach Osborne. It's a little dry sometimes, but it's appreciated. He's a funny guy, a lot of fun."

Osborne's humorous characteristics are something Adam Treu enjoys telling his NFL teammates about.

"I told the guys about Coach Osborne's wonderful sense of humor because no one knows about it," Treu said. "When they named January 'Tom Osborne Month' in Nebraska, I saw where he said, 'Well, I hope my taxes don't go up.' Because remember when they named that highway after him near his hometown [Hastings], he got a speeding ticket. People have been able to see that he really is a funny man."

Treu said Osborne was at his comedic best when trainer Doak Ostergard was around.

"Doak and Coach Osborne go back and forth all the time," Treu said. "I found some photos of Doak doing something or another, nothing big, but they were older photos and that's really what made them funny in the first place. Coach Osborne was working out and I took the photos to him. He was doing the treadmill. I showed him the photos and he started smiling. He said, 'Thanks, I'll put these to good use.' He gave them to Mike Grant, I think, and Mike superimposed something on them, pasting into a really funny picture. Coach Osborne put them up and everyone got a good laugh about that one. Even Doak."

Mike Minter said Osborne's smile and wit was infectious.

"Every time Coach Osborne would laugh, it would really get to me," Minter said with a smile. "Every meeting, like at the FCA [Fellowship of Christian Athletes] meetings, he'd make five or six jokes and have the audience laughing so hard they were just dying."

A phone call from Osborne during Grant Wistrom's senior year in 1997 led to one of the more comical memories Wistrom had.

"Without a doubt, he's got a great sense of humor," Wistrom said. "He calls the other day and he was giving me a hard time on the phone. He has a nickname for my roommate. I was acting like my roommate; because sometimes I don't like to talk on the phone. He's really a funny guy. Anybody who is around the program knows he's got a great sense of humor."

Joel Makovicka said the upperclassmen especially enjoy Osborne's wit.

"It's a thing where, as you get older, he becomes more of a guy you can joke around with," Makovicka said. "When you're younger, you're kind of still just in awe being around him. When you get older, he's the kind of guy you can joke around with. He has a great personality and a great sense of humor. I just think he's had a lot of fun this year with this group of guys. He tries to break it up when he's in front of the team talking. It's something where, once you get older, you realize the sense of humor he's got because you're not so awe-struck any longer by him."

Like a fine wine, Osborne's jokes get better as the players spend more time with him.

"His humor is really something not many outside the program ever got to really see," Bret Clark said. "Especially when you're freshman, you're so in awe of him anyway. He's got such a straight face, you aren't sure if he's joking or serious until you get to know him. Once you get to know him, he's very funny."

Ahman Green is reserved, not unlike Osborne. Therefore, Green had a keen appreciation for Osborne's occasional quips.

"In terms of humor, his is kind of like mine. I do crack some jokes here and there," Green said. "He's not a comedian. He works hard here to be a coach. If he comes across as stoic, that's because it's his job to be a coach. But he does crack a joke here and there."

Aaron Graham said many fans would have really enjoyed Osborne's sense of humor.

"That's absolutely true," Graham said. "I really think that if Coach Osborne is asked, confidentially, who he enjoyed coaching the most, he would probably say Christian Peter. Christian was one of those guys who was one in a million. You know Christian always had a smart-aleck comment or a line he'd throw in whenever he could and that would get the players laughing. But Coach Osborne could talk Christian Peter's game. Christian would make a smart-aleck comment and Coach Osborne would fire an even funnier one right back. You could see the intelligence Coach Osborne possessed because he was always a step ahead of all of us, especially when it came to that kind of thing."

While Osborne's sense of humor showed through more publicly during his final years as the Husker coach, the players said he always was that way.

"He's really closed to the media a lot of times and for good reason," Jared Tomich said. "But he has a great sense of humor. He'd razz the defense in practice. He'd say, 'The offense is going to run the ball down your throat. Strap it up and get ready to roll.' He had a really dry, honest sense of humor."

The humor would often come at odd times. However, it served to break up the monotony or it allowed the players a smile during serious moments.

"He would make a joke when you would least expect it—just out of the blue," Michael Booker said. "We'd be preparing for a big game and out of his mouth would come a punch line."

Jamel Williams said most in the nation will never know that Osborne really did have a good sense of humor.

"Not everyone, especially outside of Nebraska, knows how funny Coach Osborne is. He has a great sense of humor," Williams said.

Osborne was not the kind of guy who would pass on funny stories or tell jokes. It was an intellectual sort of humor that came from an honest man.

"He's not a back-slapper guy who will tell you jokes," Dave Rimington said. "But he's very intelligent and picks up on things quick. You're really something if you can get one past him."

Terry Connealy agreed that Osborne's sense of humor was derived from a sense of intellect, not from his funny bone.

"Coach Osborne's got a great sense of humor, but you have to be on your toes to catch it," Connealy said. "There's definitely a side there that some people never had the pleasure of appreciating. And for those outside Nebraska, it's a real shame they never saw that side of Coach."

# CHAPTER 12

# FROM LINCOLN
## TO THE NFL

*T*he players develop a deep feeling for Tom Osborne while they are in Lincoln. However, as the geographical distance separating the former players from Lincoln grows, so does their affection for Osborne and the program at NU.

"You appreciate Coach Osborne even more after you get away from the program," Mark Traynowicz said.

Offensive lineman Adam Treu was part of both national championship teams and was drafted by the Oakland Raiders after the Huskers won the Orange Bowl over Virginia Tech, culminating a two-loss season in 1996.

"Of course, I look back fondly at my time at Nebraska," Treu said. "We won a majority of our games—all of them two years in a row. That was the hardest adjustment for myself in the NFL, losing so many games."

The Raiders fired head coach Joe Bugel after Bugel's first and only season as the head coach in Oakland.

"Those coaches at Nebraska have been there for so long and that's really helped the program have all that success," Treu said. "In the NFL, there's so much pressure on coaches and owners. If they don't win or show signs of improvement, they are out. I've learned that firsthand. I learned in my first year in the NFL that the league is a business."

Treu said there is at least one parallel between NU and the NFL.

"At Nebraska, whether or not you are getting playing time comes down to how you execute on every play in every game, and every play, every day in every practice," Treu said. "In that aspect, it is the same as the NFL. Because in the NFL, there's always someone to replace you. And sometimes, when you're replaced in the NFL, you're off the team quickly and out of a job, at least in some cases."

The whole approach players must take in the NFL is different from the structure Adam Treu had grown used to at Nebraska.

"There are so many things I learned from Coach Osborne, I could go on all day," Treu said. "I'd have to say the most important thing is the work ethic. I see that a lot more now that I've left Lincoln, especially after having a down season with the Raiders. There were some people on the Raiders who let their egos get in the way. At the University of Nebraska, you see such a structured program. There you play for pride and your school, not because you are getting 'X' amount of dollars to play on Sunday."

The hardest part for Brenden Stai when he left Nebraska for the Pittsburgh Steelers was the family atmosphere that Osborne and his staff worked so hard to maintain.

"The NFL is a brutal business, but it is still exciting," said Stai, noting that his pro coach, Bill Cowher, is a players' coach. "One thing I really noticed when I first came to the NFL was that I missed all my buddies. All the guys here are married, have their own lives and often live far away from Pittsburgh. You are teammates with them and count on them; but when the season ends, that's it, they are all gone. It wasn't like that in college. And in the NFL, the guy next to you could be gone the next day, because it is a business."

Donta Jones, a linebacker for the Pittsburgh Steelers, said the NFL is a quantum leap from college football.

"The biggest difference is that you have to learn things a lot faster in the NFL and the game itself is a lot quicker," Jones said. "The mental part is different as well. We'll learn seven different defenses in one meeting here [in Pittsburgh]. At Nebraska, we'd learn one in a meeting, work on it, go through it in practice and learn it before we'd go on to adding another."

In some ways, Jones said, the Huskers were like an NFL team because there are no major professional teams in Nebraska.

"Nebraska is somewhat like an NFL team, because the closest professional team isn't even in the state—it's the Kansas City Chiefs, three hours away," Jones said. "The fans in Lincoln treated us very well. It was like a big NFL team out there."

While Mike Minter experienced immediate success in the NFL starting at defensive back as a rookie for the Carolina Panthers, he knows the NFL is at the opposite end of the football spectrum from college football in Lincoln.

"It's definitely different in the NFL," Minter said. "It is a business. And you have to take the attitude that it is, in effect, a business."

Mark Traynowicz said even the practices in Lincoln are run better than in the NFL.

"When you're at the University and you grow up a Nebraskan, you just expect the coach to be around a long time," Traynowicz said. "He does everything right, even in his own life, not just coaching. I went off to play in the NFL and had coaches who weren't that great. Coach Osborne was very organized. When he blew a whistle during practice, you knew where to go to. When I went to Buffalo, there were times that no one knew what was going on. That helped me really understand what Coach Osborne did. He truly cares for his players. Until you're a player, you don't know how honest he is."

One of the NFL's shortcomings—the concept of team—is something the players realize is a cornerstone of Nebraska's success.

"He instills a team concept," Bret Clark said. "I was lucky enough to go play in the NFL for a couple of years. You don't realize it when you're playing for him, but then you go out to the NFL and you don't see that team concept. You see that individual stuff, because that's what most of the other college programs are like. When players from a lot of the other colleges get to the NFL, they don't know the team concept. You don't cut down your players and coaches in the media. You work it out among yourselves. In my view, that's the biggest reason Nebraska's program has stayed on top. That and no coaching changes, which Coach Devaney started and Coach Osborne maintained and brought that level up even higher. Because kids nowadays are even harder to keep together."

Like Jared Tomich, Steve Forch went from playing for Osborne to Mike Ditka.

"Playing for Coach Osborne was different than playing for any other coach," Forch said. "His style is more analytical than emotional. At times, it was somewhat challenging playing for him. He didn't want you to get too emotional. He wanted you to focus your energy. He was very effective in that way, making sure you knew what your assignment was and not getting lost in the emotion. Playing with the Bears was a whole lot different, because I played for Mike Ditka."

The experience of playing for Osborne is as memorable as it is unique, according to St. Louis Rams guard Zach Wiegert.

"It's not the same in the pros or high school," Wiegert said. "Playing for Coach Osborne at Memorial Stadium was the greatest."

Michael Booker said he hears horror stories from his Atlanta Falcons teammates about their college days. Booker said he knew he had a good situation in Lincoln, but that it did not sink in until he made it to the NFL.

"In the NFL, players talk about some of the stuff that goes on at colleges when they recruit players," Booker said. "I never experienced any of that bad stuff when I went to Nebraska."

After hearing players in the NFL talk about their college experiences, Jared Tomich was more grateful than ever for how he grew in Lincoln under Osborne's wing.

"All the players have the utmost respect for Coach Osborne," Tomich said. "I've seen and heard about when a coach comes into a team meeting or into the locker room and players are still gabbing or joking around. When Coach Osborne came into the locker room, he always had our undivided attention right away."

All-Pro guard Will Shields of the Kansas City Chiefs, who played for Osborne from 1989-91, echoed that sentiment to reporters the day Osborne resigned.

"His demeanor was so different from any coach I ever had," Shields said. "He was always calm and reserved. Most coaches do most of the talking. He just let the work come out of you instead of trying to force the work out of you."

Broderick Thomas has enjoyed success in the NFL in spite of playing on four different teams.

Despite the constant state of transition he finds himself in, he still steps right in when he joins a new team without missing a beat. He points to what he learned at Nebraska as the reason for his continuing success.

"What has enabled me to keep playing is what I learned at Nebraska and from Coach Osborne," Thomas said. "For me to go everywhere I've been and start has been a blessing from the things I learned at Nebraska. In Lincoln, I learned good footwork, knowing where to be, where to keep my hands—all the fundamentals. The whole Nebraska philosophy is that each player has to handle his own responsibilities on every play. If you learn that in college, you can play anywhere in the NFL."

Few former Huskers experienced as much NFL success as Tom Rathman, at least when it comes to winning Super Bowls and being consistent.

"I think about the whole experience," Rathman said. "It's a great institution and a dominating football program—Nebraska has everything. When you play for one of the best coaches in the country, it carries over into your professional career. You know how to handle success."

Dean Steinkuhler also developed a deeper affection for Osborne's words after Steinkuhler had left Lincoln.

"One of the things he said that stands out was, 'This is the greatest time of your life,'" Steinkuhler said. "I didn't realize it at the time because I was hoping to get to the NFL to see how great it was there. But then after the NFL, I looked back at Nebraska: There was Coach Osborne, how people there treated me, from coaches to trainers—and it is just unmatched. It was just a shock to me when I got to the NFL. Coach Osborne was right, but I guess I didn't realize that until I went to [NFL] training camp."

The difference in poise between Osborne and NFL coaches left a mark on Steinkuhler.

"A couple of times I remember we hadn't played very well in the first half and he wasn't uptight," Steinkuhler said of Osborne. "You go to the NFL and there are some very uptight coaches. Even

Coach Osborne's assistants were the same way when things went bad. There wasn't any screaming or yelling at the players. It was always business as usual."

Marc Munford said he never met another coach like Osborne while he was in the NFL.

"He's just the kind of guy who is the consummate leader," Munford said. "He instilled ideals, values and work ethics in everyone, not just his players, but the assistant coaches and other people around him. People just fed off of that. He's just a real solid individual."

The Huskers not only dominate on the field, but off the field as well, according to Mark Traynowicz, who said he takes pride in the way both current and former Huskers don't seem to let their mouths get them in trouble.

"You could kind of look across the country at different coaches and their players," Traynowicz said. "Coach Osborne's players as a whole—both in the NFL and while they are still in college—don't seem to say the wrong thing at the wrong time. Even on the field, playing at Nebraska, there's never much talking going on. Things have changed a little bit, there's more talking than ever on the field. But at Nebraska, it's still not that way. Coach Osborne didn't like end zone celebrations after touchdowns. He was like, 'Why do you want to celebrate? You should expect to be there. Don't act like it's unusual. Score, and move on.' "

# CHAPTER 13

# TAKING A
# BEATING IN THE
# MEDIA

*N*ewspaper headlines and television sound bites were vicious toward Coach Tom Osborne and the University of Nebraska at times, especially during the march to back-to-back national championships in 1994 and 1995. The players took the criticism as hard as anyone because they believed the media's presentation was one-sided and told only half the story.

The players got to the point where they took the criticism directed at Osborne personally.

"That does tick you off a lot," said Chris Dishman. "No one knows him like we do. It really hurts. It's like someone saying something bad about your father. We stick up for him as much as we can. The bad part is that people only see the one side because of the media."

"I never thought the scrutiny was fair," Tony Veland said. "The easy thing for a coach to do when a player has a problem is to just abandon the player. That makes the coach look good to the media because they think the coach has rid the program of a problem. But what does that tell the young man? What does it tell others who are thinking about going to that college?"

"Exposing" Osborne was an ill-fated attempt by the media, said Jared Tomich, who played from 1994-96. Because Osborne was never really known to the national media, it was easy for them to take shots at him. However, had they seen Osborne the way the players had or if the media had even come to Lincoln—since, in many cases the editorials and TV news shows were done from a time zone or two away—the stories would have included a lot more depth about what Osborne believes.

"A lot of times, it seems like the media feels it has to expose him; but with Coach Osborne, there's nothing to expose about him,"

Tomich said. "People tried to do that to him for the wrong reasons. The media made it seem like he didn't mind having troublemakers. He was as troubled by what happened as anyone. He just cares about his players in a fatherly kind of way. He's like a father who knows his son did something wrong, but he's not going to hang his son out to dry. He wants everyone to do things to the best of their ability."

Zach Wiegert remembers a lot of college students getting in trouble. However, if they didn't play sports, not only was their problem not reported in the media, but the student might not have had the support needed to address the problem.

"Everybody thinks Coach Osborne is soft on everyone," Wiegert said. "He's not soft, just fair. You have to understand that the average college kid makes mistakes. If that kid doesn't play football, nobody notices when they do something wrong. At a successful program like Nebraska, everything is under a microscope. The public doesn't see that millions of college-age kids made mistakes over the years."

Osborne did not give second chances to help the football team win. Rather, he offered second chances to help the players have a shot at life.

"Coach Osborne believes in second chances," Veland said. "He is about giving people opportunities they would not get if they didn't know him. The presence he has about him is kind of indescribable. His Christianity and honesty will always be remembered. He stuck his neck out at times for players and put himself on the line to save the players from having their lives turned upside down."

Simply dismissing players from school would have let the player off the hook. Instead, Osborne demanded that the player step forward and address the problem in addition to dealing with and learning from the consequences of his actions.

"What would it have done to throw the players who had problems off the team? He told them that what they had done was not OK," Tomich said. "He made sure they understood that and took responsibility for what they did. He didn't want those incidents to be the end of the line for those players. He knew they would have a future after they were done playing football. Keeping them in the program made them be accountable for their actions. What would they have done if he would have kicked them out of school? He gave them a chance to rehabilitate themselves and learn from their mistakes."

Veland said that accountability is critical for the players and society in general.

"Coach is an honest person. He'll stick his neck out for people and they see that," Veland said. "A lot of coaches, when their players get into trouble, will just run the player out of the program. But Coach Osborne wants to help the students grow as people. If they make a mistake, he's not happy about it. But rather than run them off, he'll make them accept the consequences for what they did, and he will help them move forward and put it behind them so they will learn from it and not make the same mistake again."

While the Lawrence Phillips situation (Phillips was suspended from the team after assaulting his former girlfriend and reinstated for the last regular season game and the Fiesta Bowl) and others through the years gained a lot of national attention, former Husker defensive back Mike McCashland said similar situations arise every day in the real world.

"There's always going to be problems in society," McCashland said. "They seem to show up every day in sports because it is magnified by the media. There are a lot of second chances given every day in life, but we don't hear about that. If a player did something wrong, Coach Osborne tried to rectify that so hopefully the player can get on the right track."

The media's commando mentality demonstrated by Bernard Goldberg on the CBS program "48 Hours" really hurt the players the most. Goldberg set Osborne up during the Phillips incident, asking Osborne if the coach would allow Phillips back on the team had Phillips assaulted Osborne's own daughter.

"I think it's very unjust," Wistrom said. "That guy from "48 Hours" doesn't have a clue. He had no idea what the situation was.

Coach Osborne treats people fairly. You look at people like Riley Washington, who was acquitted, or found not to be guilty. Riley could have missed out on a whole year of football. Coach Osborne is a very smart man. He knows what is best. He knows his players better than anyone else does. Anybody who thinks that he meddles too much is an idiot and I'll blatantly say it to their face. He does what he thinks needs to be done. And 99.9 percent of the time, it is the right thing."

Jamel Williams said the media's approach is uniform—shoot first and often never ask the meaningful questions.

"That's just how the media is," Williams said. "They like to build you up higher than you really should be and then bring you down more than they should."

The players fully support the way Osborne handled the Lawrence Phillips situation.

"We had a clean program there," Booker said. "Every program has problems and we had to deal with our own, too. No one is perfect. But when we had a problem at Nebraska, since we were winning national championships, the media really tried to take it to us. Some of the things they reported were true, but they never got the whole story. Or, if they did, they didn't tell the whole story. The way Coach Osborne handled Lawrence Phillips was the best way possible. He kept him in the program and made him look at what he did. His attitude was that Lawrence had to pay for what he did, but Coach was not going to let it destroy his whole life."

Matt Davison said growing up in Nebraska, he had heard about the problems, especially in 1995. However, he never wavered in his support of Osborne. And when he arrived on campus as a freshman in 1997, he found out he was right.

"I remember reading everything in the newspapers about how he runs a dirty program and the players he brings in are criminals— things like that," Davison said. "I didn't believe it before I was here. And now, it just makes me angry. Along with everyone else here, I feel like he's the best person I've ever met in my life. Head to toe, from his heart, I just have so much respect for the man that it makes me hurt to know that he was treated that way. I hope he's not remembered for that. I don't think he will be, but it was just very unfair the way he was treated."

Mark Daum said the way the Phillips case was portrayed by the media was bad in two ways. First, it took the focus away from everything Osborne had done over the years. Second, Osborne did, in fact, handle Phillips the best way for everyone involved.

"It's really sad the way the national media looked at Coach Osborne in terms of just a few discipline cases the past few years," Daum said. "That is so far from the truth as to what Coach Osborne is about. In Phillips' situation, if he would have kicked him off the team, Phillips might have gone back to Los Angeles and gotten into more trouble. Coach Osborne wanted to give him a chance at life. Because of how he was brought up and the environment he was surrounded by when he was younger, the only chance at life for Lawrence Phillips came from the structure in the football program. If the media knew Coach Osborne better, that would change the way they feel about him."

Former players would not second-guess the way Osborne handled any problems. Instead, their unwavering faith in Osborne told them that the coach would do the right thing for every one involved.

"I was away from the program when they had those situations during the second national championship season [in 1995]," Rimington said. "So I got only second-hand information. I trust Coach Osborne and I have faith in him. I know he's not going to put someone out there on the field who is not deserving to play."

The win-at-all-costs label pasted on Osborne by the national media, especially during the 1995 season, troubled the players the most.

"A couple of years ago, he was being portrayed as someone who would do anything to win," Jason Peter said, "and that's not the case with him. It's always a matter of he's going to do what he has to do to get a person help. If they follow through with his rules and what he requires out of them, he'll give them the opportunity to play again. The way he was portrayed was kind of negative and that's one of those things where he overcame the things people were saying about him. That's one of the reasons why I look up to him so much."

Even the harshest player suspensions were justified, according to Jason Peter.

"Without a doubt, he has treated us fairly," Peter said. "A couple of the players that have been in trouble over the last couple of years . . . it's certainly been fair the way he handled them. Whether it was with one who had to sit out six or seven games of the season and had to go and get treatment and stuff like that . . . I wouldn't argue with the way Coach handles these situations. He's a man of morals, and whatever he feels is right, I would definitely agree with him."

Another factor the media overlooked was the judicial process itself. To condemn a player based on unsubstantiated allegations— which, in several cases, was applicable because often the player had charges dropped, sometimes within a week or two—flies in the face of the American system of justice.

"He does trust his players," Rimington said. "And there is something called due process. You can't just pull a guy off a team because of accusations. For a lot of those guys, football is a very big part of their life. To take them off based on shaky allegations is not right."

Dean Steinkuhler said Osborne not only made the right decisions in keeping those players in the program but made the morally correct choice as well.

"If Coach Osborne kicked those kids off the team, they wouldn't have had to be accountable to anybody," Steinkuhler said. "A lot of guys come in from single-parent families. Coach Osborne was always there for them. The last five or six years, you can really tell by how the players talk about him, how he has stuck his neck out for them—you can see how much that means to them when they're interviewed."

While the media thought that Osborne's move to keep

Lawrence Phillips on the team was to increase the team's potential for success, Broderick Thomas claims that Osborne was trying to give Phillips a chance and, at the same time, give society a chance at having a mentally healthy Lawrence Phillips.

"Lawrence, or any other player who made a bad decision, could have just been a disaster to society," Thomas said. "With the help of Coach Osborne, and his ability to see within the person and try to find a chance to help them, those players can right their wrongs. Coach Osborne is able to see the good in everyone. That's the reason he gave them the second chance. Other coaches might just look at the negative part of that player. That's half of the problem with criminals in America. They make that first bad decision and it's a devastating blow to the rest of their lives. They leave the structure they have and their life is basically over as they continue in the wrong direction. Coach Osborne's belief is to help the player learn from the mistake so he won't repeat it. Sure, that helps the player— that second chance. But it also helps everyone else in that player's life or anyone he is going to come into contact with in the future."

Aaron Taylor said all Osborne did in holding out the possibility of a return to the team was encourage the players to grow up and be responsible. The media's portrayal did not give that impression, Taylor said.

"I think it was totally unfair," Taylor said. "He does anything and everything for us student-athletes. When he was just getting pounded by the media . . . it wasn't fair. I mean, he was doing everything that he possibly could in order to help those guys out. He can't watch them all of the time. They have to grow up some time in their life and he was trying to help them grow up. And yet he was trying to get them help. There comes a point in time where you just have to say, 'Hey look, you need to grow up by yourself.' You can only do so much, and unfortunately, some guys didn't respond to that and it looked bad on Coach Osborne. But he was doing everything he could."

While the media focused on Phillips and other high-profile players, it never chose to find out that Osborne had the same rules for all of his players.

"I know he treats his players fairly and that's exciting to see, because a lot of places around the country treat their players with preferential treatment, especially their star players," Taylor said. "Whether it was a walk-on or a star player, he treats them all the same."

While the national media reported its perception of the story, the Husker players said they knew what was really going on every step of the way in 1995.

"There are a lot of things that are said in team meetings that never reach the papers," Aaron Graham said. "Not something in a negative aspect, but everything was out in the open to everybody on the team, whether it was Lawrence Phillips' case or whatever. Nothing was kept in the dark. Coach Osborne let everyone know what his intentions were. When Lawrence's thing first happened, Coach Osborne said he didn't know what happened and that he hadn't made up his mind yet. He always kept us informed. He never made a rash decision. It was never like that."

While Graham did not agree with some of the decisions his teammates made off the field, he completely supports Osborne's decision at every step.

"I absolutely, 100 percent agree with him and the way he sticks with his players," Graham said. "You have to remember that he brought us to Lincoln to get an education, first and foremost. Playing football always came after that."

Graham said Osborne knew the risk of simply dismissing players and taking away the support system in place at the University.

"When things didn't go right," Graham said, "Coach Osborne was always willing to give a second chance. Because he knew the outcome of people denied that opportunity and that the consequence of not giving a second chance far outweighed the risk of giving them another chance and getting them the help they needed."

Marc Munford also was disheartened by the media's approach.

"I disagree wholeheartedly with that win-at-all-costs label they stuck on him in 1995," Munford said. "Anybody who can do what he does at that level is a winner. Show me someone who likes to lose. He's definitely a competitor who wants to win. But to win at all costs? No way. That is ridiculous to say that about him. The national media has always kind of had a bone to pick with the program and Coach Osborne."

Toby Wright plays for the St. Louis Rams, so he knew about Lawrence Phillips before the Rams drafted him. The Rams released Phillips during the 1997 season and Phillips went to the Miami Dolphins. While Phillips seemingly continues to struggle with his conduct, Wright said Phillips would have had no chance to get his life together without Osborne.

"Of course, he's always been there for his players," Wright said. "He was always a sort of father figure, regardless of what happens. Of course, he has always been that way, even before that happened with Lawrence [Phillips] and the other things that year. I was not surprised [by] the way he handled Lawrence. For Lawrence and the others who had problems, it was really a blessing to have someone like Coach Osborne there for them."

Every few years, there are a couple of players who stepped outside the rules. Bret Clark said the problems were magnified in 1995 because of how good the Huskers were on the field, coming off a national title and heading toward a second one.

"I was upset because that's not how it was," Clark said. "He just tried to give everyone a fair chance. He explains the situation to every player. You either abide by the rules or you are gone. Most of the players I knew straightened themselves up. I knew five or six from 1982-84 who had that problem."

Clark said Osborne saved Phillips from a life of who knows what.

"Look at Lawrence Phillips," Clark said. "That kid had nothing to go to."

What got lost in the translation from Osborne to the media and then to viewers and readers was the context of why Osborne handled situations the way he did.

"It's real easy for people to sit back, read the paper and think they know everything about the problems they [the players] went through," Jobman said. "In reality, that helps you know nothing. For all the years I played there, when we had the problem and I read about it the next day in the paper, I'd be like, 'Where did they get that story?' It had some truth to it, but you never got the feeling for what was really happening. So you end up with 95 percent of the people reading about it and they don't really know what's going on. Yes, they have some facts, but sometimes those are screwed up and there are other things involved that you never will read about. Like what happened with Lawrence Phillips: What he did was wrong, really wrong. But Coach Osborne approached it as a Christian, thinking about what was best for everyone and making Lawrence answer for what he did. Would Lawrence have gotten counseling and had to own up to what he did if Coach would've thrown him out of the program? I don't think so."

Rimington said he would have liked to see the media figure out that Phillips was not needed to help the team win in 1995. Additionally, Phillips did not play in the games in which many thought the Huskers would have needed him most, including a late-season contest at Colorado.

"As far as the Lawrence Phillips situation is concerned, if anyone watched the Florida game, which was the only game where he saw any real action after he was suspended, they didn't need him anyway. Coach Osborne had the guts to stand up and make the right decision."

While the media made it seem like Osborne let players off the hook, John Parrella believes the opposite was true—that Osborne's decision to keep players in the program kept them from running and hiding from their actions.

"Coach Osborne's approach was to rationally correct problems," Parrella said. "That's how I was raised. Coach Osborne is there to help you and make you responsible, not kick you out the door. I don't think it was fair the way the [media] tried to hold him responsible for everything the players did, especially off the field.

Coach just wanted you to do your best. He taught us how important it was to know right from wrong. And if you made a mistake, he made sure you were held accountable."

The media which criticized Osborne did not have a grasp of the big picture, something Turner Gill said was important to keep in mind.

"I know a lot of people who wouldn't have given a lot of guys a second chance," Gill said. "It would have been, 'OK, forget about him, let him go, let him move on.' But instead, to show you how sincere Coach Osborne is with his players, he wants to help them out for our society. It's not all about football. He wants the kid to change that behavior.

"He's there for the person in the long run, not for a short period of time," Gill said. "That's what people in the media don't really understand. It's very easy for all of us to say, 'OK, the kid did something wrong. So let's get rid of him and move on.' But that's not going to help the kid and it really isn't going to help our society. That's where I've really learned and see what Coach Osborne does. He truly loves the young men on this campus."

The perception that especially bothered players was that Osborne kept players around to help the team's chances of winning.

"Anyone who says Coach Osborne is a 'win-at-all-costs coach' or [that he] 'harbors felons' is pretty ignorant," Terry Connealy said. "Anyone who knows him at all knows that the last thing you'd see among his priorities is to win football games at all costs. That's the last thing he'd ever do. I don't put much stock in the people who talk that way about Coach Osborne. They obviously don't know the man."

Troy Dumas, who came to NU from Cheyenne, Wyoming, said that while Osborne did not show it publicly, he always made it clear to his players that anyone who didn't follow the rules would be held accountable.

"He would be upset if we were out doing wrong, but he never turned his back on us," Dumas said. "He gave us an opportunity to correct the wrong and made sure we became stronger people and more responsible in the process."

Had the public known all the considerations that went into Osborne's decision to reinstate players after suspensions of varying lengths, Cory Schlesinger believes they would have understood and supported Osborne's decision about players who got into trouble.

"Definitely, the media never got the whole story or even got it right in a few cases I can think of," Schlesinger said. "I think people have to figure it out for themselves—who Coach Osborne is and what he stands for. Some people outside the program don't understand everything going on and everything that went into Coach Osborne's decision."

Sheldon Jackson said the media never figured out that Osborne believes he is responsible for his players, whether they do something good or bad.

"In the past few years, I think that he has been mistreated," Jackson said. "People think he goes out and recruits thugs and hoodlums to come play football here. Unlike most programs, Coach Osborne is going to give individuals second chances. He sees the good in each individual. He brings them in here and allows that good to be opened up and broadened. He gives second chances. He believes in everybody's goodness. I think the media should acknowledge that as a good trait that Coach has and praise him for that aspect, instead of trashing him for it."

Mark Blazek never took the stories in the media seriously. Since he knew what was going on "inside" the program, he did not worry about the perception being presented by the "outside."

"The media, in my opinion, is looking for the story that sells papers," Blazek said. "They don't have a clue. If you know Coach Osborne, or have any steady contact with him, there was nothing to those stories about him being a 'win-at-all-costs coach.' Those stories were a joke."

Mike Minter said he believes the players had a harder time dealing with the media criticism of their coach during the 1995 season than Osborne.

"It's very difficult to read what was written or watch what was on TV, especially when you know the type of man he is," Minter said. "The people who wrote about him in a negative way didn't even measure up to him. They talked bad about him without understanding what they would have done in the same situation. It's easy to write a criticism of what someone is doing when you don't have to do it yourself. He handled it like no other man could. He withstood it all and that's part of why he's a legend."

Ahman Green said the media never got to know Osborne. In turn, that led to many around the country not being able to understand the coach's reasoning at times.

"Especially during my freshman year [1995], it was a wrong, slanted look at Coach Osborne that was totally off of how he is as a person," Green said. "I don't see how the media could portray him as playing felons and stuff like that. That's totally the opposite of who Coach Osborne is. He's a players' coach and he helps his players, no matter what."

Something else Green does not think should be overlooked is that not only did Osborne follow his own moral compass, he also stayed within the boundaries of the law and NCAA rules.

"You can only go so far in terms of what you can do for your players," Green said. "With the situation that developed my freshman year with Lawrence, Christian and Tyrone [Williams], he handled them real well. He didn't step beyond any boundaries. He stayed within them real well. He stayed within the context of college football and NCAA rules. He never broke any of the rules. He did what he could and he did that real well."

# CHAPTER 14

# THE BIG RED
# BEGINS LIFE
# AFTER OSBORNE

*T*he day they heard Osborne had resigned, players and former players did not worry much about the future of Nebraska football. They knew Osborne's system would continue and that success would follow. While the players were all happy for Osborne, they also realized a special era had come to an end in Lincoln, because a special man was leaving the school and the program upon which the entire state shared an emotional investment.

"I'm happy for Coach Osborne because he obviously wanted to do something else with his life and spend some time with his family," Dean Steinkuhler said. "Coaching is so time-consuming. The only sad thing for me is that my boy won't get a chance to play for Coach Osborne. I would have liked that. But things can't go on forever."

Tommie Frazier is not worried about the future of the program. He says the years of experience on the coaching staff will add up to another national title run—year after year.

"The guy who is succeeding him has been there 20 years," Frazier said. "They will be fine. I'm not surprised he's stepped down. Twenty-five years is a long time to coach. It was just his time."

Many programs experience, at least initially, a slip when an established coach steps down. That drop is sometimes sustained when another transition quickly follows. However, none of the players expect that kind of scenario for Nebraska.

"Whenever you lose a man like Coach Osborne—who is not only a good person, but a good football mind—that will impact the program," Harry Grimminger said. "But the one thing you hear is that the transition will be smooth and be in capable hands. If any place can absorb the loss of someone like Coach Osborne, it is Nebraska. Coach Solich is a good person and a good football coach.

You see places like Alabama and Miami drop off when they change leaders. That won't happen in Lincoln."

Broderick Thomas, who became a member of the Nebraska Football Hall of Fame in 1994, echoed Steinkuhler's sentiments: That his only regret in seeing Osborne leave is that his son won't get to play for Osborne.

"I tell my 7-year-old son, 'little' Broderick, that it was just great to have played for Coach Osborne," Thomas said. "I don't want my son to play football; but if he did, I would introduce him to Nebraska before any other college program."

Like others, Mike McCashland expects little change, at least at first. However, there is still little doubt that Solich will have the chance and obligation to make his own mark at Nebraska.

"I think because you have such a strong figure in Coach Osborne, there will obviously be some changes," McCashland said. "It's just the respect that he gets from everyone and the assistant coaches. You never get that respect until you earn it. Frank Solich will do a heckuva job. There's no doubt he'll get the job done."

Randall Jobman, a Husker from 1987-89, said the Big Red will still make a big mark on the national rankings each year.

"I don't think you'll see a lot of change," Jobman said. "Since I've been there and have watched this thing progress, Coach Solich has assumed a larger role. It's my opinion that when Coach Osborne was getting older, he passed a lot of responsibility on to Coach Solich. I think what you see today is that a lot of success comes from Coach Solich and the assistants. Granted, anyone taking over will try some things differently and do some things the way Coach Osborne might not have done them."

Since the assistant coaches handled a lot of the recruiting, Jobman does not expect to see much of a dropoff in the talent level.

"In recruiting, you won't see some wholesale things," Jobman said. "Sure, high school players will miss the chance to play for Coach Osborne. I doubt Nebraska will actually lose that many recruits just because he has retired."

Turner Gill, the one-time quarterback turned NU quarterback

coach, said Osborne's decision to leave is respected, but Gill admits he took it with a heavy heart.

"The day I found out, it definitely was a sad day—no question about it—or a sad week, even," Gill said. "I guess we could try to do the things that he did in the way he did it. But there's only one Tom Osborne.

"We're going to miss him from an aspect that he was a great coach," Gill said. "But we're going to miss him more as a person. He was a much greater person than he is a coach. I know there are some people who find it hard to even believe that. But not everyone gets to see the human part of him. I'm going to miss him dearly on a daily basis, just talking with him and learning from him, not just about football, but as a human being.

"He is a role model for kids and society," Gill said. "That is going to be missed. I'm sure he's going to be somewhat involved still and try to do some things to help the community, because that's just his nature and part of his spiritual belief. He's in this to help the young people in our society."

Former Husker center Aaron Graham, who joined Randy Schleusner, Jake Young, Dave Rimington, Mark Traynowicz, Pat Tyrance, Grant Wistrom and Trev Alberts as Husker Top-8 Award winners, the highest honor bestowed on a student-athlete by the NCAA, said he expects Solich to survive the early growing pains of succeeding a legend like Osborne.

"Coach Osborne has been a coach at Nebraska since I was born," Graham said. "All I can do is maybe compare it to the stories I've heard about when Coach Devaney retired. It wasn't necessarily all roses for a while for Coach Osborne at first. It takes some time to get used to that new role and make adjustments. That's what Solich will go through. Coach Osborne and everyone really have a lot of respect for Coach Solich. I like the way Coach Solich 'brings his lunch to work every day.' By that I mean that Coach Solich comes to work every day to bring you everything he's got. He pushes his players to the limit every day. Look at the productivity he got out of his guys. It's unmatched."

Matt Davison said the coffee shop chatter will be overwhelming, but the changes in the program won't be.

"I think this off-season, people are going to talk about the upcoming season, talk about how it isn't going to be the same," Davison said. "Once next year comes around and we keep winning, I don't think it's going to make a huge impact on the fans. Like I said, he's not going anywhere, he just won't be in the meetings and in charge all the time. As far as the fans go, they can expect the same thing out of the Nebraska Cornhuskers."

Like Davison, freshman Bobby Newcombe took the news of Osborne's decision to resign hard on December 10, 1997.

"I feel pretty bad about it," Newcombe said. "But then again, I understand fully why he chose to take this time and I understand that, with the things he's been going through, he does need the rest."

The eventual retirement of many of Osborne's long-time assistants will give Solich one of his biggest challenges, McCashland said.

"Keeping the assistant coaches together as one is what makes this work," McCashland said. "If we can do that, there won't be a problem. But you have to remember that Charlie McBride, Milt [Tenopir] and George [Darlington] are all right there, near the end of their careers. There will definitely come a time where we'll have to bring in two or three new coaches at one time. So there might be some change. I don't believe that will be immediately or that the program will be a whole lot different. It is a well-oiled machine right now and it will continue to move forward.

"In a way, it may be kind of exciting to see someone else making the calls and to see how things shake out," McCashland said. "But it is going to be odd. I go to most of the games. I went to every one this year except the opener against Akron. Next year, it'll be strange to look over there and not see Coach Osborne."

San Diego Charger defensive lineman John Parrella said the program will continue to move forward. Moreover, Parrella said everyone owes it to Osborne to continue to support the current coaches.

"We're losing a great coach, an outstanding person. I could go on about Coach Osborne for an hour," Parrella said. "At the same time, I don't see it hurting the success the team will have, especially not in the near future. In Coach Solich, they have someone who has been there a long time. It will always be a very high-class program. You have to look at it in the way Coach Osborne would—that we need to support Coach Solich and the team."

Ahman Green is more worried about the fans than the football team when it comes to life after Osborne.

"We have a good coach coming in, in terms of Coach Solich," Green said. "How will it impact the state? I don't know. I don't know everyone, so I don't know how they would feel or how they will act. But team-wise, there should be no letdown at all."

Chris Dishman said he remembers Coach Solich as a detail-oriented coach who ran the players hard in practice.

"I don't think a whole lot is going to change," Dishman said. "Coach Solich is a hard worker. He's the one who pushes practice very hard. He would bust our butt on the running station at practice. He pushed it pretty hard. That's the kind of coach he is—he's pretty demanding. I don't see any drop off. It's Nebraska—we just find someone and reload."

St. Louis Rams linebacker Troy Dumas said Osborne will be missed, but the legacy will continue in Lincoln.

"I think the ball will keep rolling," Troy Dumas said. "Coach Solich will do a heckuva job. He's been around there long enough to know what's going on. He'll do a good job. I can't see where there would be much of a fall off. But the whole state and the program will miss Coach Osborne."

The players from the 1997 national championship team believe they have not seen the last of Osborne. They also don't believe they have experienced the last of their success at NU.

"I don't think the program will skip a beat as far as winning football games," Matt Davison said. "With Coach Solich, pretty much all of the coaches here have a mystique about them. The character of all the coaches is about the same. So as far as this program declining in character, that won't happen. He's going to be missed by all of us. But I'm sure he's going to be around if we need him. He made it very clear that it hurt him to leave here, especially with players like myself that he just recruited last year. He would like to see us through. He made it clear to us that he was going to be here for us, no matter what. He's going to, for sure, be a part of my life and these players' lives for the rest of our days here. And the rest of our lives."

Brenden Stai said fans will quickly learn that Solich resembles Osborne in a lot of ways—both on and off the field.

"I'm not worried about Frank; he's a perfect fit," Stai said. "They won't miss a beat. He's got a lot of similar qualities. He's patient, a good teacher and has a good football mind."

Mike Minter said Solich's two decades under Osborne make Solich adequately prepared to accept the torch.

"Coach Solich has been there for 19 years, so he's ready," Minter said. "Coach Osborne knew that, which is why he probably pushed for Coach Solich to get the job."

Tight end Vershan Jackson, a co-captain for the 1997 national champion team, agreed.

"For the younger guys, you don't have to worry about not seeing Coach Osborne around," Vershan Jackson said. "He will be around to run his couple of miles a day and lift a few weights."

The feelings Nebraskans everywhere experienced when Osborne announced he was stepping down were felt by former Husker players, as well.

"I'm sure everyone in Nebraska—all Nebraska fans—were in a state of depression when he announced he was stepping down," Tony Veland, an Omaha native, said.

Jamel Williams said he knew the day would come when Osborne would step down, however, the day it happened was still a shock.

"I think it will definitely take a while for it to set in," Williams said. "The program will still move forward. Coach Solich will do a great job. He's been there for something like 20 years, and he knows the system."

Cory Schlesinger, a fullback for the Detroit Lions, was among those not surprised to see Osborne step down.

"Not really, I kind of figured it was going to happen," Schlesinger said. "I'd rather see him go out now, on his own terms, rather than because of a serious illness."

While the winning will draw a lot of the post-Osborne era focus, Zach Wiegert knows Osborne's legacy lay off the field.

"No matter if they end up winning 10 national championships in a row, Coach Osborne will be missed for his character," Wiegert said. "Winning games isn't what made Coach Osborne the greatest coach in history. It's who he was and how he went about things, how he cared for his players."

Wiegert, who won the 1994 Lombardi Award, said the decision to step down was, in its own way, another case where Osborne had the guts to make the right call.

"I'm glad he was smart enough to know when to walk away from the game," Wiegert said. "He made the right decision again."

Michael Booker, the 11th pick in the 1997 NFL Draft, did not believe it when he heard it second hand for the first time.

"I heard about Coach retiring the day it happened," Booker said. "I was in the [Atlanta Falcons'] training room. One of the media guys came in and asked me about Coach Osborne leaving and I thought, 'Uh oh, here comes another Nebraska joke.' But then I found out he was serious. I was like, 'No way.' But it is what Coach Osborne wants to do and I'm happy for him."

Solich was a good choice to replace Osborne, the players said. Equally important was the decision the cadre of assistant coaches made to stay with the program.

"The level of play won't be affected that much," Booker said. "Coach Solich and the assistants will still be there and they'll pick it up right where Coach Osborne left off."

Joel Makovicka will miss Osborne. But he knows Solich well and believes a new era is dawning in Lincoln, one that will have the same kind of success, values and positive impact that it had under Osborne.

"If you ask the question, 'How do you replace arguably the greatest coach of all time in college football?' [The answer is] to get the next greatest coach in college football, Coach Solich," Makovicka said. "I've had the privilege to be under Coach Solich the past few years. Coach Solich has instilled the same thing Coach Osborne has instilled in all the players and that is the work ethic and the values."

Solich will be a change from Osborne, Bret Clark said. But that's a good thing, something Clark said Osborne will likely encourage— that Solich make his own mark, his own way on the program.

"It will still go in the right direction," Bret Clark said. "I think you'll see a more vocal person in Coach Solich. But you'll see the same type of play-calling and levelheadedness as time goes on."

Choosing a current assistant coach was important, Thomas said.

"I don't feel the loss as much because of who he's turning the reins over to," Thomas said. "Whether it was Charlie McBride or Frank Solich, it would be like Coach Osborne is still there in a sense. The assistant coaches respect Coach Osborne so much. They know and helped build the tradition and know how to deal with and handle the players. It's always been done a certain way and I don't think that will change under Coach Solich. In that regard, I feel that Tom is handing it over to a new living legend in Coach Solich."

Had Solich not been in line to succeed him, Munford wondered if Osborne still would have chosen 1997 as the time to step down.

"I think it was key that, at least indirectly, he was able to basically name his successor," Munford said. "That was a key instrument in letting him make the decision to step down without turning the cart over. He was able to keep the stability in there. All the assistants have been there for a long time. I'm sure there will be an impact. I don't know if it will be felt immediately. I really don't think they should miss a beat as far as the program moving forward."

The solid foundation of the program and the direction Solich will provide along with the cadre of longtime Osborne assistants will prevent any slip in the program.

"I don't think there will be much of a drop-off," Mark Blazek said. "I see that as a tribute to what Coach Osborne and his staff have accomplished. I'd be really surprised if there was much of a drop-off. Most of the coaching staff is still there. A lot of those guys were there when I was playing. I don't think anything there will change. Coach Solich has a lot of the same characteristics as Coach Osborne. I have a lot of respect for him."

Grant Wistrom, the 1997 Lombardi Award winner, an award which goes to college football's top lineman, said Solich's selection as Osborne's successor should make the transition smooth.

"Without a doubt, he is going to be greatly missed," Wistrom said. "As far as a letdown in football, a letdown in recruiting, a letdown in support, or the players not playing as hard—that's not going to happen. Coach Solich is a great coach. He's been here long enough. He knows the ins and outs of Nebraska football, how important walk-ons are to the program, how important recruiting outside of the state is. The players already here really like him. He's one of my favorite coaches on the staff. I can joke around with him. I'm not afraid, if I have a problem, to voice it to him. And if he's got a problem, he'll voice it to you, too. I think it's very important, the communication between the player and coach. And we definitely have that with Coach Solich. So I don't really see any letdown."

Wistrom said in the unlikely event Osborne was to enter public office, he'd have one vote for sure—Wistrom's.

"Obviously, people are going to be sad and rightfully so," Wistrom said. "He's an icon in this state. If he wanted to run for governor, he would probably win. I know I would vote for him. He's got more morals than probably anybody in government right now."

Aaron Taylor said many will only get a full appreciation for what Osborne accomplished and how he went about it, now that Osborne has stepped down.

"He has set a standard for a lot of coaches around the nation," Taylor said. "And possibly for Coach Solich, too. Maybe Nebraska fans around here will appreciate what they had. I think Coach Solich is going to come in and do a great job without a lot of change, just like Coach Osborne wanted it. It's going to be exciting the next few years."

While the direction and success of the program aren't likely to change any time soon, the very appearance of Nebraska football has undergone a facelift.

"What will be strange is to not see Coach Osborne on the sideline anymore, chewing his gum and with his eyes squinted," Booker said. "I remember when I was a player, I thought, 'Doesn't that look ever change?' Then, I watched a game on TV this year and I was like, 'No, that's the same look. I know it well.' He's always so calm and poised."

Dave Rimington, a 1983 inductee into the Nebraska Football Hall of Fame, believes the continuity is the important factor. Osborne is a tough act to follow and anyone would find the challenge of filling such a living legend's shoes to be enormous.

"Coach Osborne leaves a legacy of excellence in everything he's done," Rimington said. "He's done a great job. I believe he had the opportunity to help pick his successor, although it wasn't all his decision. It was Athletic Director Bill Byrne's decision. Coach Osborne felt Frank Solich has the qualities to keep the program going. That's a great thing. Coach Devaney picked Coach Osborne and Coach Osborne has kind of picked Coach Solich."

Jason Peter said that while Osborne will be missed, the coach has earned the right to pursue his life off the field at this point. And with a personal and coaching resumé second to none, Osborne can look back with no regrets.

"It's going to be sad that he's not going to be around," Peter said. "But he's done everything possible that a coach can do. He's won national championships. He graduates his players. He has All-Americans. He's done everything, really, so it's time for him, I think, probably just to enjoy himself. It's hard on somebody's body, all the frustrations and stuff that goes along with being a head coach. He's earned the right to sit back in a log cabin and fish for the rest of his life."

Moving the program forward will be easier than letting go of their deep emotional attachment to Osborne, according to the players.

"There is going to be a little bit of him that people are going to hold on to tightly, so it won't be as if he has completely left us," Sheldon Jackson said. "But we are getting a 'new' head coach who has been in the program for 19 years, so there's not going to be a slack off in any way, shape or form. Coach Solich has been here and he can get the job done, just like Coach Osborne can. I'm looking forward to playing for Coach Solich and seeing what we can do next season."

While the players know the program will continue to move forward, they also know that a new day is dawning for Nebraska football as Osborne leaves the field for the final time.

"With Coach Solich beginning a new era, it's a positive thing," Peter said. "Coach Solich is a great coach and he's going to do well for the program."

Peter has just a few words to say about Osborne, but they speak volumes about how the players feel toward their coach.

"I will always remember," Peter said, "that he was a great coach who stood for all the right things."

Wistrom echoed the sentiments, then took them a step further.

"It's going to be a great loss and people are going to feel it," Wistrom said. "He's obviously going to be remembered in this state and with good reason. Probably throughout the nation, people are going to talk about one of the greatest coaches in history—Tom Osborne. He's going to be gone, but not forgotten."

# EPILOGUE

*T*hese columns were written by Bob Schaller while he was the sports editor of the *Scottsbluff (Neb.) Star-Herald* from 1991 to 1997. Schaller covered the Huskers' back-to-back national championship seasons in 1994 and 1995.

## OSBORNE 'CELEBRATES' HIS FIRST NATIONAL CHAMPIONSHIP, JANUARY 1995

Fewer than 12 hours after the biggest win of his illustrious coaching career, Tom Osborne stepped to the podium Tuesday morning. He smiled slightly, as he always does, and he began to answer questions about his No. 1 Huskers' 24-17 win over No. 3 Miami the previous evening, a game that assured Osborne of his first national championship.

He opened his mouth and said the unthinkable—at least to those who do not really know Tom Osborne.

"I don't really feel any different than after last year's game," Osborne said, referring to the 18-16 Orange Bowl loss to Florida State that cost the Huskers the national championship. "If we get a trophy at the end, that's icing on the cake. But trophies fade kind of fast. We have a bunch of trophies in Lincoln that people don't look at anymore. I'm more concerned with the whole process."

The national title is a sure thing at this point. David, even though he had a higher ranking, slew Goliath in Goliath's own backyard. That is no small feat when it is a pick-a-Florida college playing on its home turf on New Year's Day.

The "new" kid—to be sure, a big kid long before last night—on the block is Nebraska, a school, the coach explained, that is more concerned with the process. That's Tom Osborne. Those few in the audience who knew him at the Orange Bowl media headquarters smiled. It has always been about the process. It was Tuesday. It will be tomorrow. It will be forever, or as long as the closest thing the Midwest has to a modern-day folk hero continues to lead the Big Red.

Osborne's crowning glory, the national championship, will come after this morning, only two days after Osborne showed the country that he can play alphabet soup with the best of them. Osborne called the right Xs and Os at the right time, and in the process ended a seven-year bowl-win drought for Nebraska.

The score is mere happenstance to Osborne. The national title for Osborne is simply the result of the process, when it works to near perfection.

"Sometimes, I feel more down when we win and we don't play well," Osborne said matter of factly.

Would the college football pollsters recognize the Huskers for playing better than Miami, had NU lost? No. But that's what makes Osborne the icon that he has become.

Husker defensive coordinator Charlie McBride was smiling from ear to ear about the process as Osborne spoke.

"If you worked for Tom, you'd understand everything he's done," McBride said. "Tom would rather see a kid graduate than play football. He's done a heck of a lot for the community that no one hears about. It's not just about football for Tom."

The national championship will be awarded to the Nebraska Cornhuskers today. Osborne will be recognized as the best in the land.

It's something we, in Nebraska, have long known.

## REFLECTIONS FROM THE
## 1995 ORANGE BOWL, MIAMI, FLORIDA

*What was it like?*

That's the question of the day after Nebraska was voted national champ following Sunday's 24-17 win over Miami in the Orange Bowl.

After four hours sleep over the course of 2 ½ days and a bumpy flight home, everyone I saw when I got back asked, 'What was it like? What was it like to be at the Orange Bowl?'

Less than a minute after the scoreboard clock read 0:00, Nebraska 24, Miami 17, I was with Osborne on the field when NBC's John Dockery interviewed Osborne about what it felt like to be the national champion. I was being pushed into Osborne's right side as a Florida State Trooper kept me pinned in, and the rest of the crowd out, as Osborne told the world how it felt to win the Orange Bowl Sunday night.

Here comes that answer, and more.

**Pregame**

Seeing the Orange Bowl from my hotel, the Airport Marriott, was quite a feeling after seeing it so many times on TV. I took the 4 p.m. shuttle to the game, thinking I could hit the media tent for free food. Just as soon as I hit the press box, I was besieged by members of Miami's electronic media who wanted someone from Nebraska's media to go on their shows. The most fun about that was doing a radio show with Kim Bokamper, the former Miami Dolphin, on the Hurricanes' station. I think they wanted me on because that station had done the Dolphins' playoff game the day before and needed a scouting report on Nebraska.

I said to forget all the talk about this and that . . . focus on whether Miami could run the ball against the Blackshirts. If the 'Canes couldn't run, they couldn't win. One on-air bet had me putting up some Nebraska beef—my favorite—against some south Florida crab, which, I reasoned, would look nice on the side of a plate next to a big T-bone steak.

Miami ended up rushing for 29 yards. I will be out front in sub-zero Nebraska weather waiting for the UPS guy and my package of crab.

*What was it like?*

Nebraska falls behind by 10, and the other writers around me are having a field day, saying Brook Berringer should have started in place of Tommie Frazier, this after Frazier was intercepted.

After Nebraska blew a chance to tie the game when Berringer was picked off in the end zone, Frazier was put back in. A writer just in front of me, from Washington, said Osborne should have stuck with Frazier the entire game. All of these "experts," and not one of them had ever won a college football game—as a coach, or player.

When the fourth quarter started, I decided to head down to the field. I started organizing some thoughts in my head about whether I'd do a "We tried hard" column or one about New Year's Day nightmares. As I hit the field, Frazier handed the ball off to Cory Schlesinger, who went in for a touchdown. I never knew Schlesinger had the ball until I heard a collective gasp from the 'Cane faithful behind me. After Frazier hit Eric Alford for the two-point conversion, I wanted to turn around, rip off my imaginary helmet, and do some funky rap dance in front of the Miami bench and fans—a la the 'Cane players. Better judgment prevailed and I kept my head—probably literally.

*What was it like?*

The Husker defense, which must have eaten enough Wheaties to send Post stock through the roof, played its heart out. That's an old cliche´, but it really is true. So many times, the Blackshirts could have quit, especially after the offense fumbled and then, one series later on first and goal from the Miami four, the Husker offense threw an interception.

After every play, Ed Stewart and Christian Peter were among those yelling about making "one more play." They were yelling this, even on first and second down. The strategy was to neither look down the road nor fret on the offensive miscues. The plan was to focus on one play at a time, taking care of business and beating back the ghosts of Big Red New Year Day's past every time Miami quarterback Frank Costa yelled, "Hut!"

*What was it like?*

I'm standing next to Drew Goodman when Schlesinger scores the first of his two touchdowns. Goodman is a TV play-by-play guy and had a radio show for the Denver Broncos. Goodman is an old friend.

"I know I'm from Colorado, but I want Tom Osborne to win a national championship," Goodman said.

As Goodman speaks, the unspeakable—the unthinkable—is happening right in front of us. Miami punts and Frazier moves the Big Red up the field at the speed of light. My gosh, when Schlesinger goes into the end zone for a second time on the same trap play, in front of all that Husker Red in the end zone, my heart is thumping in my throat. The goose bumps have gone up on both of my arms and over my scalp. I feel like I should be running or something. It is at that moment that I realize I am no longer "from Colorado," and that I am a born-again Nebraskan.

*What was it like?*

I'm over in front of Nebraska Governor Ben Nelson. I have a thousand Clinton jokes that I finally have a chance to tell him. But all I can do is wave to him and say how great this is, this religious-like experience that one can only understand from knowing what Nebraska and Osborne's Huskers put up with, from the Nebraska jokes to the constant bias from the media.

The clock is winding down and the bench is winding up. My gosh, little old me, in a tie and suspenders . . . I feel like I should be holding that white helmet with the red "N" up in the air, as though it is some sort of flag that the country had darn well better get up and salute.

*What was it like?*

Terry Connealy sacks Costa. Kareem Moss picks off a pass on the next play. The clock is winding down. I wonder if I should be this close to Dockery, because everyone else is near him, knowing that sort of proximity will get their face on TV for one historical moment.

The crowd is counting down the clock from 20 seconds. I run as hard as I can to the other side of the Nebraska bench, opposite Dockery. This ended up being a great move, because the folks around Dockery trying to get to Osborne are getting acquainted with a host of Florida State Troopers, who, like the rest of greater Miami, carry semiautomatic weapons.

A state trooper is on my left. I hold up my press credential and the trooper nods, which I think either meant I was OK or he was going to kick my fanny anyway. I run alongside Osborne and Dockery is shouting, trying to get Osborne to stop and go on the air.

Osborne insists that he must see Miami coach Dennis Erickson first.

*What was it like?*

Osborne won't let the players pick him up just yet. No, we will win with the same class that we had when we lost in the past.

We get to the handshake with Erickson and the crowd descends as Osborne and I get a little closer than either one of us probably ever hoped. I am so proud that I want to hug Osborne. But I know, as a journalist, there are simply some lines that can't be crossed.

As I run off the field with the players, the fans—the best ones in the entire world—are screaming out not just their praise, but their true affection for the players, the coaches, the state and what it all stands for.

We are running hard, trying to get away from the crowd. I slow down to catch a few players and watch Osborne. All the guff he's taken over the years. The class he's always shown to everyone. The way he always—ALWAYS—insisted on doing everything the right way.

You want to know what it was like? It was like a Rocky Mountain high at sea level. It was as though all the pain, from all the years of disappointment, had been washed away. It was like the good guys—the ones in the white hats, albeit with a red "N" in this case—had finally won.

It was a bazillion jolts of electricity running through the nervous system. It was what Utopia was described as in books.

It was something I will never forget for the rest of my life.

As I stopped and stood on the hallowed turf of the Orange Bowl, I watched Tom Osborne run.

Into history.

## CAMP CONTROVERSY: NU VS. CU, GAME 8, 1995 SEASON

BOULDER, Colo.-We're here on the road as Camp Controversy sets up shop at Folsom Field Saturday.

The former starting I-back, who was suspended for assaulting his former girlfriend, didn't play. That was contrary to a media feeding frenzy that there would be a Lawrence Phillips sighting.

*Camp Controversy.*

The coach, who keeps the program on track and catches heat because he believes in second chances and redemption, ho-hummed his way through another post-game press conference. Tom Osborne excused himself if no one wanted "anything else."

Actually, no one really wanted anything else after Saturday's 44-21 romp over Colorado.

What else is there to want?

"We can't control a lot of things," said Husker wingback Jon Vedral. "All we do is win football games, because that's all we can control."

*Camp Controversy.*

There's Tommie Frazier, who deserves the Heisman Trophy more than anyone else. Politics have a lot to do with the award. That's OK. While some overrated, padded-stat running back (former Colorado Heisman winner Rashaan Salaam comes to mind) is sitting at home spit-shining the Heisman, Frazier will have to be content preparing for another shot at the national championship in Arizona at the Fiesta Bowl.

*Camp Controversy.*

What issues will arise this week? It doesn't matter. Because if nothing else comes up, there's still the Phillips thing to rehash time and time again. Certainly, Phillips deserves any punishment he gets from the court system—and the university. However, he's still a 20-year-old young man. And if this country doesn't believe in second chances, the problem goes a whole lot deeper than the Phillips' case.

*Camp Controversy.*

Did Nebraska win by enough points Saturday? Again, does it matter?

"We've heard a lot of negative things," said Husker rush end Grant Wistrom. "You guys hear it, too. A lot of people try to move us down in the polls. But we beat a good team today. And we beat them convincingly."

Look at the scores from Saturday and you'll see that Kansas State, the same team that Nebraska pummeled last week, beat previously undefeated Kansas.

"Everybody can say what they want," said NU safety Tony Veland. "We'll just keep on winning."

But that won't help the Huskers this week. No, you don't get prorated points in the polls unless your north-south field is located east of the Mississippi (Florida State and Penn State come to mind). No, the way it will work is that no matter how bad the Huskers beat Kansas—and they will, make no mistake about it, clobber the Jayhawks—it won't be enough.

Because Kansas is no longer undefeated. And it matters none that it came at the hands of a team, K-State, that the Huskers destroyed all of seven days ago.

*Camp Controversy.*

A different week. A different city. A different Top-10 opponent. But the same result.

*Camp Controversy.*

It's coming home this week for Iowa State, heading to Kansas the week after and then wrapping up the season with Oklahoma in Lincoln.

"We finally got really tested," said NU senior rover back Mike Minter. "I think we passed the test. And we don't really care about what everyone else thinks."

*Camp Controversy.*

Where only the strong survive.

## NEBRASKA 37, OKLAHOMA 0, 1995 REGULAR SEASON FINALE

LINCOLN—Really, there weren't that many questions.

Nebraska Coach Tom Osborne quickly finished his post-game

press conference after the No. 1 Huskers moved to a perfect 11-0 with a 37 0 beating of rival Oklahoma.

It was the last game ever in the Big 8, with the Big 12 on next year's horizon. A big win.

But a bigger game lay ahead.

A showdown for a second straight national championship in the Tostitos Fiesta Bowl awaits Nebraska. If Florida beats Florida State today, it's Nebraska and Florida—two undefeated heavyweights—slugging it out for the national title in the Arizona desert.

So any excitement Osborne had over going undefeated during the regular season for the third year in a row was either tempered by the upcoming bowl . . . or maybe something else.

Could it be the beating both he and his program have taken from the national media this year?

Could it be the Heisman Trophy hype that obviously weighed heavily on his quarterback, Tommie Frazier, during Friday's game?

Or could it have been Tom Osborne just being Tom Osborne, which isn't enough for the national media, but is plenty enough for the Heartland's most respected citizen to get up each morning and look himself in the mirror?

The answers: Maybe, no and definitely yes.

Tom Osborne is always going to be Tom Osborne. He wins neither for sustenance nor the spoils. He wins because of "the process."

To be sure, winning is a by-product of the process. And that process means bringing recent high school graduates into his system, defining roles for them, letting them grow into their roles, and then watching them leave the university, degree in tow, as men.

That doesn't have to mean winning, even though it ends up being a win nearly nine out of every 10 times.

"I really appreciate the attitude and effort of this football team," Osborne said. "This year's team, I'll remember for many reasons."

He didn't elaborate.

He didn't need to, either.

Because this year's team, while perfect on the field, wasn't perfect off of it. Imagine that: kids acting like kids at times.

Now, make no mistake, Lawrence Phillips' beating of an ex-girlfriend was a crime against society, and Phillips will pay for it, wearing a label the rest of his life for a crime against the opposite sex. There is no excuse for what Phillips did.

But these journalists who decried Osborne's handling of the Phillips' case, and the other handful of Huskers who still, like many college-age young men, need guidance to distinguish right from wrong, never knew the whole story.

Because they don't know Tom Osborne.

This is a man who lives his life by the Bible. The writers who lambasted him accused him of condoning the beating of women, when in fact nothing was further from the truth.

That is, Osborne was sickened more than anyone who, from hours and time zones away, did the trendy thing and wrote about what an awful beast Osborne had created.

Still, Osborne faced many of those journalists at the post-game press conference—the ultimate professional. He holds no grudges and points no fingers because he believes in the Golden Rule of doing unto others . . .

Yep, won the Big Eight, he said, without much of a smile or emotion in his voice.

Yep, headed for Arizona and the Fiesta Bowl, he said, allowing himself a grin.

Yep, he's proud of this team not for what it could do, but for what it has done.

What Nebraska did involves winning. The problem is, these very journalists who tackle Osborne like an unblocked blitzing linebacker view winning as something on a scoreboard.

The writers and broadcasters who do nothing but glorify a touchdown run slammed Osborne, claiming he doesn't care about these athletes as people.

Yet these same journalists rarely give us a glimpse of the human side of these young people, using a highlight reel to define a personality, and then chide Osborne for allowing a player a second chance.

Tom Osborne headed down an empty stairwell in South Stadium, likely to change clothes and spend time with his family.

Back in the media room, young men were given Greek-god status by many of the same journalists who took shots at Osborne from a distance.

The bandwagon was boarding for the Fiesta Bowl, and everyone wanted a front-row seat.

There will be betting in the millions when the Huskers roll into Tempe, Arizona, for a chance at another national championship.

But there is one bet that will go unwagered, and for good reason, for it is a sure thing:

Tom Osborne will keep being Tom Osborne, believing in the power of the human spirit while making sure those under his charge are held accountable for their actions.

There is no question about that.

## The 1996 Fiesta Bowl, Tempe, Arizona—Back to Back

"Hi, my name is Bob."

"Hi," the support group answers in unison.

"Like I said, my name is Bob, and I'm a Husker-aholic."

I am in withdrawal after returning from the Fiesta Bowl. Everyone keeps asking what it was like to be on the field when Osborne and Nebraska repeated as national champions. You really want to know? I mean, do you really, really, want to hear the whole thing? OK, get your coffee and let's get to it.

### The week before

Arriving a week before the game seemed a bit silly. Watching the sportswriters around the country practice their trade was downright hilarious, if not ridiculous. Media Day at SunDevil Stadium was hysterical. Writers would often ask the player a question, and then not write anything down when the player answered. I thought that was odd. Then, the writer would take the player down a road, with leading questions. The writer would scribble furiously when he got "the quote" he wanted, often disregarding the "positive" part of the story in search for the "juicy" part that would sell more papers or, even worse, help the writer justify writing something negative. Using part of a quote, when done incorrectly, takes the comment out of any context from the pretense under which the answer was given.

I can't stop thinking about one high-profile newspaper writer, who also does some TV reporting. He kept trying to get Husker rush end Grant Wistrom to say that Wistrom would have to drop back into coverage more often than usual against Florida. Wistrom handled it well and was patient. I finally chimed in that Wistrom had yet to drop back into coverage—that rush ends at Nebraska were basically the equivalent of defensive ends, not outside linebackers, as this writer had thought rush ends to be. I said that the media, since they were assigned to cover the game, should at least respect the game enough to do its homework. I read about every Florida game and saw several on tape in addition to studying all the accompanying stats.

The writer gave me the look of death as if to ask, "Who are you to point out that the media should respect the event it is covering?" The big-time writer didn't like me. Not only did I sort of like that, but I would get used to more and more of that in the following days.

## The ESPN crew

Media Day was made for me when ESPN Game Day host Chris Fowler started talking to me in the stands. When he saw my name on my media badge, Fowler asked, "You aren't the Bobby Schaller who played high school hockey for Air Academy High School?"

I told him that I was. It turns out I played against Chris and his little brother, Drew.

Drew was really good and Chris wasn't bad, either. By this time, ESPN's Mike Tirico and Craig James were hovering around me, so I got to meet them, too, just because my team played Fowler's Palmer High School squad. That made me feel good. Plus, a lot of the boneheaded sportswriters who I had taken on were in the vicinity. They had to sit through the whole conversation, which must have been sickening for them!

Fowler was a great, great guy. The ESPN crew was completely professional. James' dad was very ill, yet James' insight was some of the best the whole week. The writers are jealous of TV journalists, for different reasons. First of all, the TV job appears easier to a writer, than the writer's own job. Plus, the TV reporters, at least in major markets, make more money than the writers. Also, the TV guys were more "cosmetically correct" for the most part, while the sportswriters looked like they were waiting for someone to drop a donut. In 10 years of sportswriting, I couldn't have imagined ever getting excited about meeting someone in the media. But Fowler and his crew, especially after seeing them in Lincoln in 1994, were just great. Down to earth and very engaging, they were the one bright spot—aside from the Huskers, of course.

## January 1, 1996

Boy, I can't tell you how much it meant to me to hear the writers talk about all the places they went drinking the night before—I went to the gym at the motel on New Year's Eve. I realize at this point that not only do I not fit in with most of the sportswriters, I don't want to be a part of what they represent. All that drinking at so many bars . . . how many of these writers drank and drove? Of course, that won't make the paper. No, we've got much bigger fish to fry, these writers must have reasoned, so they went after the Huskers.

A somewhat comical scene developed after the final pregame conference when Tom Osborne and Steve Spurrier posed for pictures together holding the national championship trophy (the most recent two are now on display in Lincoln, for those of you scoring at home). The newspaper photographers there were looking for any new kind of photos, instead of just the "mug shots" they had been taking all week.

The photographers started pushing—really pushing—each other, and Osborne said, "We don't need the media getting into a fight."

I was sitting right in front of Osborne and Spurrier, in the front row, apparently in the photographers' way. No one in the media had asked me politely to move, so I didn't. After hearing Osborne's comment, I said, "Don't worry about it coach, if they get into a fight, it wouldn't be in the paper." Osborne looked me in the eye, and allowed himself only a grin. Another dozen dirty looks came my way from the media. You know, I realized at that moment that I would save a king's ransom on Christmas cards in 1996.

## The game

OK, OK, I don't like the print media. But the game—well, that was something else. I take on all comers in the press box. I see Jay Marriotti from the Chicago Sun-Times. He was in Denver when I was in Fort Collins. He asks my opinion of the Phillips things and offers no judgment, except a nod, when I tell him. Even though I just accidentally made a friend in the print media, I'm still in a good mood.

Besides, I always liked the way Marriotti bucked the establishment and took shots at other writers. So, with absolutely no due respect to Kravitz and the others, maybe I'm on the right track after all.

Some really cool woman named "Mitzi"—from the Fiesta Bowl committee staff—is in charge of my press box row, and she likes the Huskers. Some bozo writer from Sarasota, Florida, who picked Florida to win in a big way, won't even look my direction, even though in the second quarter I walk in front of him a half-dozen times stating, "Wow! Who'd have thought it would be this big of a romp!"

I am getting dirty looks left and right and I am awaiting the first invitation to "step outside." The Huskers continue to crush Florida. The 29 second-quarter points start coming when Husker outside linebacker Jamel Williams tackles Danny Wuerffel in the end zone. Williams would later tell me that he wasn't even supposed to blitz on the play. But when the lone running back emptied out of the backfield in motion before the snap, NU middle linebacker Doug Colman, lined up over the Florida center, waved Williams in. The rest is history, much like Florida and all the prognosticators who picked Nebraska to lose.

Come the second quarter, me and Mitzi are on cloud nine. When NU cornerback Michael Booker intercepted Wuerffel and went all the way for a touchdown, the press box went silent—until I said out loud, "Wasn't Booker supposed to be picked on?"

I am in shirt and tie, with matching suspenders, while many writers don't respect the event enough to even wear a shirt with a collar.

All week long, Florida had hid its hand, and wouldn't divulge its game plan or any tricks it had up its sleeve. Nebraska, on the other hand, said "We will run the option, and Florida won't stop us. We will cover man-to-man in the secondary, and Florida won't beat us. We will blitz Wuerffel, and they won't stop us because they haven't seen a rush like our rush this year. We will stop their run."

What a show of bravado—Nebraska came right out and told Florida what was going to happen, and then backed it up with a 62-24 rout. As the game wound down, I was on the Husker sideline. As the clock wound down and a Gatorade bath became apparent, I circled in front of Osborne to avoid getting soaked (it was actually chilly on the field that night).

## National champs–again

As it turned out, I ended up—not altogether by accident—right next to Osborne for the second year in a row. I ran across the field with him for the post-game handshake with Spurrier.

After that was complete, Osborne turned to go get the national championship trophy. I started rounding up the players—that ended up being GREAT, because a lot of writers either stayed in the press box to file (and wait for quote sheets) due to the late start, or went to the interview tent.

So I talked to 19 players on the field. They had only Spurrier for a while in the interview tent. I knew what Nebraska had accomplished was very special. Sadly, I also knew that most of the country wasn't going to get the whole story in the right manner because I had, unfortunately, got to see the "best of the best" sportswriters in action. And let me say this right now: If that is the "best of the best," then I will be more than content to be one of the "best of the littles"—either that or I will leave newspapers altogether.

Anyway, after I talked to Tyrone Williams, Chris Dishman, Aaron Graham, Phil Ellis, Christian Peter, Eric Stokes and Michael Booker, I saw Ahman Green. But a tug on my shoulder stopped me in my tracks.

"I've been looking for you," said Husker rush end Jared Tomich. A lot of things went through my mind—like my life, for example— as I saw nothing but a big No. 93 in front of my face. "I wanted to thank you for what you did the other day."

Here Tomich and I were, with the "hometown" Nebraska crowd screaming and yelling, Osborne getting the national championship trophy, and Tomich wants to thank me. He was referring to the last day of interviews. The writers were down his throat and I jumped in, "Does anyone want to ask a football question? I mean, did anyone come down here to talk football?"

That dispersed a lot of the writers that day. Tomich had gone on to talk about the positives that came from a very negatively presented story in a national magazine about Tomich's Attention Deficit Disorder. Few writers were scribbling when Tomich spoke his heartfelt comments. But they must not have thought those would sell papers or make for the kind of headline they wanted.

So, back to the scene.

I have a great chat with Tomich on the field. When I head to the interview tent out back of the stadium to get quotes from Osborne and Phillips and Frazier (the only two players I needed, but didn't get on the field), I sit in front of, ironically, Tomich and Aaron Graham. Both smile and mouth "Hi" as I elbow my way into the front row.

The writers have deadlines to meet so they are being more rude than they normally are, interrupting every one of Osborne's answers to interject another question. I raise my hand, showing Osborne the kind of respect he always afforded me. Of course, he calls on me right away, addressing me with a smile as "sir." Osborne repeats my question so everyone gets the context and then says how the seniors did a heckuva job this season.

I run back to the press box and begin typing madly. I have two computers going, sending through the phone lines with one, typing on the other, sending with that one, switching the two, and keep going. No—not every reader of other newspapers is going to get the coverage that this deserves. But, dang it, my readers have too much invested in this team, this state—what it all stands for—to be hung out to dry. I will go until I have nothing left, just like the Huskers did—until my scoreboard, a midnight deadline, says I am out of time.

I had 13 stories in the following morning's paper. I felt like I should have had a couple more. But when I heard the writers around me complaining that they had just finished their first or second story at midnight, I knew I had done my job.

There was no doubt the Huskers would win—none at all.

Back in August before the march to a second consecutive national championship began, I had written in my column that the Huskers would go undefeated, win the Fiesta Bowl, and after the Fiesta Bowl, "there would be very, very little debate as to who the best team in the land is."

I walk out in the cold Tempe night. Husker fans are honking, up and down Mill Street. I want to high-five every one of them. Nebraska has been, and will continue to be, an island unto itself, both geographically and intellectually.

That's fine with me. Because we don't want the outside coming in and making our place more like their place already is. Some in the nation, who got only half the story—and it was a tainted half, at that—rooted against Nebraska. The national media, a great, great majority of which never visited the state, never interviewed the people about whom they wrote, chastised the very fabric of our character. But those who knew the whole story—the truth—cheered long and hard for the Big Red that night.

It mirrored the kind of life we here in the Heartland live. The storms before harvest are vicious, and it doesn't always seem fair at times. But we persevere to see the light of another day. And with that day came another national championship.

## The 1997 National Champion Huskers
## Osborne's Last Team

Dan Alexander
Derek Allen
Luis Almanzar
Eric Anderson
Josh Anderson
Travis Antholz
Sean Applegate
Erick Arens
Rod Baker
Matt Baldwin
Sasho Becvarovski
Jason Benes
Tom Beveridge
Mic Boettner
Dion Booker
Kris Brown
Lance Brown
Mike Brown
Ralph Brown II
Correll Buckhalter
Ben Buettenback
Grant Bunton
Jamie Burrow
Tim Carpenter
Kenny Cheatham
Monte Christo
Jeff Clausen
Josh Cobb
Tyler Cotten
Jon Coyne
Eric Crouch
Matt Davison
T.J. DeBates
Luke Denney
Billy Diekmann
Brandon Drum
Mitch Ebke
DeAngelo Evans
Demond Finister
Clint Finley
Eric Fischer
Jay Foreman
Pat Friesen
Russell Froehlich

Scott Frost
Paul Fujan
Lonnie Fulton
Jay Gates
Ben Gessford
Marcus Giles
Bobby Gill
Nick Gragert
Ahman Green
Mike Green
Matt Grummert
Chris Gustafson
Billy Haafke
Dan Hadenfeldt
Brad Hamik
Brandon Harrison
Aaron Havlovic
Kyle Henson
Josh Heskew
Russ Hochstein
Quint Hogrefe
Matt Hoskinson
Matt Ickes
Julius Jackson
Sheldon Jackson
Vershan Jackson
Eric Johnson
Marcus Johnson
Nate Johnson
Dave Jones
Adam Julch
Loran Kaiser
Chad Kelsay
Ben Kingston
Chad Kobus
Josh Kohl
Kyle Kollmorgen
Jesse Kosch
Bill Lafleur
Jeff Lake
Billy Legate
Curt Lenners
Gregg List
Frankie London

Chace Long
Kalin Makaiwi
Joel Makovicka
Glen Matthews
Jason McCullough
Octavious
  McFarlin
Matt McGinn
Greg McGraw
Jake McKee
Levi Mehl
Tom Milius
Willie Miller
Brandon
  Mooberry
Brian Morro
John Murphy
Bobby
  Newcombe
Jason Olnes
Tony Ortiz
Jon Penny
Jason Peter
Jerome Peterson
Hank Piening
Carlos Polk
Fred Pollack
Ryan Preister
Brandon Quindt
Dominic Raiola
Steve Raymond
Ted Retzlaff
Khari Reynolds
Brandon Roth
Dorrick Roy
Mike Rucker
Jay Runty
Jon Rutherford
Eric Ryan
Chris Saalfeld
Jason Schwab
Doug Seaman
Brian Shaw
James Sherman

Scott Siebenborn
Jay Sims
Travis Soucie
Jeremy Stanislav
Ryan Svoboda
Erwin Swiney
Chuck Tack
Jim Tansey
Aaron Taylor
Nick Terrio
Alik Tillery
Ross Tessendorf
Travis Toline
Arion Turner
Chad Tuttle
Simon
  VanBoening
Mike VanCleave
Kyle
  Vanden Bosch
Casey Vanderhoef
Mark Vedral
Dave Volk
Brandt Wade
Joe Walker
Brian Walters
Eric Walther
Brandon Wardyn
Eric Warfield
Steve Warren
Troy Watchorn
Dan White
J.P. Wichmann
Sean Wieting
Shevin Wiggins
Aaron Wills
Jason Wiltz
Grant Wistrom
Tracey Wistrom
Wes Woodward
Jon Zatechka

## LETTERMEN UNDER OSBORNE–1973-96

George Achola, 1990-91;
Joe Adams, 1979-80;
Trev Alberts, 1990-93;
Dave Alderman, 1995-96;
Leonard Alexander, 1994;
Eric Alford, 1993-94;
Derek Allen, 1996;
Jacques Allen, 1995;
Tom Alward, 1973-74;
Dan Anderson, 1973;
Eric Anderson (Omaha), 1989-90;
Eric Anderson (Lincoln), 1994-96;
Frosty Anderson, 1973;
Jeff Anderson, 1987-88;
Le Andre Anderson, 1989-90;
Marcus Anderson, 1992-93;
Mike Anderson, 1990-93;
Rene Anderson, 1976-77;
George Andrews, 1976-78;
Monte Anthony, 1974-77;
Mark Antonietti, 1987-88;
Gerald Armstrong, 1991-93;
Larry Arnold, 1994;
Al Austin, 1973;
Chip Bahe, 1987-89;
Ritch Bahe, 1973-74;
Jason Baker, 1991;
Kim Baker, 1979-80;
Scott Baldwin, 1990-91;
Tom Banderas, 1985-87;
Alvin Banks, 1991;
Bill Barnett, 1977-79;
Gregg Barrios, 1986, '88-90;
Ryan Barry, 1992;
Chris Bassett, 1996;
Phil Bates, 1980-81;
Reggie Baul, 1993-95;
Scott Beckler, 1989;
Mark Behning, 1980-84;
Vance Behrens, 1987;

Ernie Delei, 1991-93;
Jim Belka, 1974;
John Bell, 1973;
Richard Bell, 1987-89;
Trumane Bell, 1992-93;
Jason Benes, 1995-96;
Byron Bennett, 1990-93;
Todd Bennett, 1989;
Damon Benning, 1993-96;
Richard Berns, 1976-78;
Brook Berringer, 1992-95;
Donnie Bess, 1980;
Kevin Biggers, 1983-84;
Keith Bishop, 1976;
Chad Blahak, 1995-96;
Clete Blakeman, 1985-87;
Brian Blankenship, 1983, '85;
Mark Blazek, 1986-88;
Jeff Bloom, 1977-79;
Bill Bobbora, 1987-89;
Lance Bobolz, 1990;
Brian Boerboom, 1989-91;
Rik Bonness, 1973-75;
Michael Booker, 1994-96;
Pat Borer, 1983;
Randy Borg, 1973;
Jon Bostick, 1989-91;
Don Bourn, 1983-84;
Troy Branch, 1991-93;
Matt Brandl, 1981;
Lorenzo Brinkley, 1991-93;
Dana Brinson, 1985-88;
Dan Brock, 1974-76;
Kurt Broer, 1987-88;
Brian Brown, 1989-91;
Clint Brown, 1993-94;
Derek Brown, 1990-92;
Kris Brown, 1995-96;
Lance Brown, 1995-96;
Kenny Brown, 1975, '77-79;
Mike Brown, 1996;
Ralph Brown II, 1996;
Todd Brown, 1979-82;

Willis Brown, 1993;
Mike Bruce, 1980;
Paul Brungardt, 1987-89;
Tim Brungardt, 1981-83;
Dave Bryan, 1986;
Bill Bryant, 1978;
Eric Buchanan, 1982;
Peter Buchanan, 1988;
Ben Buttenback, 1996;
Dave Burke, 1982-84;
Ed Burns, 1977;
Jim Burrow, 1974-75;
Dave Butterfield, 1974-76;
Tyrone Byrd, 1989-92;
Jake Cabell, 1976;
Chris Caleindo, 1987-89;
Grant Campbell, 1981-82;
Mike Carl, 1984-85;
Tom Carlstrom, 1980-81;
Steve Carmer, 1990-92;
Bryan Carpenter, 1987-89;
Jeff Carpenter, 1975-77;
Tim Carpenter, 1994-96;
Todd Carpenter, 1985;
Chris Carr, 1984-86;
Charlie Cartwright, 1984;
Brady Caskey, 1992-94;
Dan Casterline, 1983, '85-86;
Jeff Chaney, 1990;
Kenny Cheatham, 1995-96;
Dace Cheloah, 1987;
Clinton Childs, 1993-95;
Terris Chorney, 1990-92;
Monte Christo, 1996;
Zeke Cisco, 1991-93;
Bret Clark, 1982-84;
David Clark, 1978-80;
Kelvin Clark, 1976-78;
Ken Clark, 1987-89;
John Clarke, 1990;
Jeff Clausen, 1996;
McCathorn Clayton, 1985-87;
Josh Cobb, 1996;

Tom Coccia, 1975;
Lawrence Cole, 1978-79;
Ray Coleman, 1987-88;
Sedric Collins, 1991-93;
Doug Colman, 1991,
  '93-95;
Terry Connealy, 1991-94;
Lawrence Cooley,
  1976-78;
Mark Cooper, 1984-86;
Reggie Cooper, 1987-90;
Joel Cornwell, 1991-92;
Rich Costanzo, 1974-75;
Barney Cotton, 1976-78;
Curtis Cotton, 1989-91;
Mike Coyle, 1973-75;
Curtis Craig, 1975-77;
Roger Craig, 1980-82;
Marvin Crenshaw,
  1973-74;
Jon Crippen, 1989-90;
Mike Croel, 1987-90;
John Custard, 1986, '88;
Chad Daffer, 1983-85;
Joe D'Alesio, 1989;
Doug Dalton, 1986-87;
Maury Damkroger, 1973;
Steve Damkroger,
  1979-82;
Mark Daum, 1982-84;
Scott Davenport, 1994;
Steve Davies, 1978-80;
Brian Davis, 1985-86;
Tom Davis, 1975-77;
Tony Davis, 1973-75;
T.J. DeBates, 1996;
Trey DeLoach, 1979-80;
Leslie Dennis, 1994-96;
Brad Devall, 1988, '90;
Mark Diaz, 1985-86;
Chris Dishman, 1993-96;
Jim Dittmer, 1985;
Corey Dixon, 1991-93;
Mark Doak, 1973-74;
Jim Dobesh, 1989;
Dodie Donnell, 1975-77;
Mark Dowse, 1989-91;
Chris Drennan, 1987-89;

Brandon Drum, 1996;
Doug DuBose, 1984-85;
Rich Duda, 1973-74;
Mark Dufrense, 1976-77;
Darin Duin, 1990-91;
Troy Dumas, 1991-94;
Jerry Dunlap, 1989;
Bruce Dunning, 1977-78;
John Dutton, 1973;
David Edeal, 1998-90;
Brian Edgren, 1988;
Chad Eicher, 1996;
Percy Eichelberger,
  1974-76;
Phil Ellis, 1992-95;
Monte Engebritson,
  1981-83;
Pat Englebert, 1989-91;
Gary England, 1979-80;
Steve Engstrom, 1988-90;
Darin Erstadt, 1994;
LeRoy Etienne, 1985-88;
Brent Evans, 1980-82;
DeAngelo Evans, 1996;
Al Eveland, 1974-76;
Earl Everett, 1974, '76;
Terry Eyman, 1988-90;
Terrell Farley, 1995-96;
Tony Felici, 1980-82;
Brad Ferguson, 1987-88;
Vince Ferragamo, 1975-76;
David Fiala, 1992-93;
Jeff Finn, 1978-80;
Dan Fischer, 1980;
Pat Fischer, 1973;
Tim Fischer, 1976-78;
Jason Fisher, 1993;
Todd Fisher, 1983;
Roger Fitzke, 1988-89;
Greg Fletcher, 1991;
Randy Florell, 1980;
Leodis Flowers, 1988-90;
Steve Forch, 1984-85, '87;
Jay Foreman, 1995-96;
Todd Frain, 1983-85;
Andra Franklin, 1977-80;
Tommie Frazier, 1992-95;
Scott Frost, 1996;

Charles Fryar, 1986-88;
Irving Fryar, 1981-83;
Mike Fultz, 1974-76;
Bart Furrow, 1992-93;
Ron Galois, 1985-86;
Jason Gamble, 1984, '86;
Paul Gangwish, 1985;
Randy Garcia, 1976-77;
Chris Garrett, 1988-91;
Russell Gary, 1978-80;
Reg Gast, 1976-77;
Pernell Gaston, 1984;
Gerry Gdowski, 1987-89;
Tom Gdowski, 1980-82;
Shane Geiken, 1989-91;
Scott Gemar, 1980;
Joel Gesky, 1992-93;
Turner Gill, 1981-83;
Dave Gillespie, 1974-76;
Mark Gilman, 1992-95;
Dean Gissler, 1973-75;
Robert Glantz, 1990-91;
Doug Glaser, 1987-89;
Kurt Glathar, 1981-82;
Steve Glenn, 1977-78;
Dave Goeller, 1973;
Mark Goodspeed, 1979;
Ken Graeber, 1982-84;
Aaron Graham, 1992-95;
Mike Grant, 1989-90, '92;
Lance Gray, 1991-93;
Ahman Green, 1995-96;
Charles Green, 1992;
Derrick Green, 1987;
Ricky Greene, 1983-84;
Morgan Gregory,
  1987-89;
Willie Griffin, 1986-88;
Harry Grimminger,
  1982-84;
Corey Grobe, 1988;
Danny Groskurth, 1986;
Billy Haafke, 1996;
Tom Haase, 1990-91;
Tim Hager, 1978-79;
Mark Hagerman, 1983;
Mark Hagge, 1988-89;
Jeff Hansen, 1975-78;

Brian Harchelroad, 1988;
Luther Hardin, 1992-95;
Dwayne Harris, 1992-94,
Neil Harris, 1982-84;
Ted Harvey, 1975-77;
John Havekost, 1978-79;
Hendley Hawkins,
1985-87;
Vincent Hawkins,
1991-92;
Bob Hayes, 1975;
Stan Hegener, 1973-74;
Micah Heibel, 1986-87;
Mike Heins, 1991-93;
Tom Heiser, 1974-75;
Blake Henning, 1986;
Doug Herrmann, 1981-83;
Josh Heskew, 1995-96;
Jon Hesse, 1994-96;
Mark Heydorff, 1973-74;
Todd Heyne, 1993;
Lorenzo Hicks, 1986-88;
Brian Heimer, 1983-84;
Gary Higgs, 1974-76;
Jerad Higman, 1992-94;
Dan Hill, 1982;
Jeff Hill, 1973;
Travis Hill, 1989-92;
Matt Hilman, 1991;
Curt Hineline, 1979-81;
I.M. Hipp, 1977-79;
Mike Hoefler, 1984-86;
Quint Hogrefe, 1995-96;
Erich Hohl, 1993;
Steve Hoins, 1974-76;
Brendan Holbein,
1993-96;
Tim Holbrook, 1981-82;
Tony Holloway, 1983,
'85 86;
Daryl Holmes, 1980;
Jim Holscher, 1985, '87;
Rod Horn, 1977-79;
Matt Hoskinson, 1995-96;
Corey Bill Hudson, 1987;
Tyrone Hughes, 1989-92;
Dave Humm, 1973 74;
Bill Humphrey, 1992-94;

Lawrence Humphrey,
1976;
Dan Hurley, 1979-81;
Brian Lodence, 1981;
Julius Jackson, 1996;
Sheldon Jackson, 1995-96;
Tim Jackson, 1987-88;
Vershan Jackson, 1995-96;
Jeff Jamrog, 1985-87;
Tom Janky, 1988;
Mike Jefferson, 1990;
Brad Jenkins, 1974-75;
Jason Jenkins, 1994-95;
Dave Jensen, 1990-92;
Randall Jobman, 1987-89;
Tim Johnk, 1989-91;
Ardell Johnson, 1973-74;
Brad Johnson (Harvard),
1980-82;
Brad Johnson (Ralston),
1985-86;
Clester Johnson, 1993-95;
Craig Johnson, 1978-80;
Eric Johnson, 1996;
Calvin Jones, 1991-93;
Chuck Jones, 1974-75;
Donta Jones, 1991-94;
Keith Jones, 1984-87;
Lee Jones, 1985-87;
Greg Jorgensen, 1975-77;
Mickey Joseph, 1988-91;
Adam Julch, 1996;
Ken Kaelin, 1984-86;
John Kane, 1975;
Andy Keeler, 1986-88;
Mike Keeler, 1981, '83;
Jon Keeley, 1985-87;
Chad Kelsay, 1995-96;
Erik Kiehn, 1989;
Scott Kimball, 1982-84;
Ben Kingston, 1996;
Bob Kingston, 1984;
Barry Kitrell, 1988;
Dale Klein, 1984-86;
Mike Knox, 1981-83, '85;
Tyreese Knox, 1986-88;
Greg Koellner, 1990;
Josh Kohl, 1996;

Jesse Kosch, 1995-96;
Jim Kotera, 1978-80;
Jeff Krantz, 1985;
Monte Kratzenstein,
1987-89;
Jeff Krejci, 1979-81;
Mitch Krenk, 1981-82;
John Koreker, 1986-88;
Lee Kunz, 1976 78;
Scott Kurtz, 1989-90;
Jeff Kwapick, 1980-82;
George Kyros, 1973-74;
Tim Lackovic, 1974;
Bill Lafleur, 1995-96;
Jeff Lake, 1994-96;
Pat Larsen, 1980-82;
David Leader, 1991-92;
Jeff Lee, 1977;
John Lee, 1973-75;
Oudious Lee, 1977-79;
Billy Legate, 1995-96;
Tyrone Legette, 1989-91;
Pat Lehigh, 1976;
Daryl Leise, 1990-91;
Chad Leonardi, 1973;
Mark LeRoy, 1978 79;
Randy Lessman, 1974-76;
Paul Letcher, 1978-79;
Rob Leuck, 1989;
Bill Lewis, 1983-85;
Lance Lewis, 1988,
'90-92;
Rodney Lewis, 1979-81;
Tahaun Lewis, 1987-89;
Jason Licht, 1991;
Dave Liegl, 1978-80;
Jamie Liewer, 1990-92;
Keven Lightner, 1985-87;
Ric Lindquist, 1979-81;
Steve Lindquist, 1975-78;
Dan Lindstrom, 1978-80;
Roger Lindstrom, 1983,
'85;
Bob Lingenfelter, 1974-76;
Gregg List, 1996;
John Livingston, 1994;
Scott Livingston, 1983-84;
Frank Lockett, 1977-78;

Rocke Loken, 1997;
Frankie London, 1996;
Jeff Long, 1987;
Brent Longwell, 1973;
Jack Lonowski, 1981;
Terry Luck, 1974-75;
Lance Lundberg, 1991-93;
Allen Lyday, 1981-82;
Rob Maggard, 1984-86;
Keith Makell, 1990;
Jeff Makovicka, 1992-95;
Joel Makovicka, 1995-96;
Chuck Malito, 1974-76;
Mike Mandelko, 1980-82;
Steve Manstedt, 1973;
Jon Marco, 1986-88;
Steve Markus, 1977;
Bob Martin, 1973-75;
John Martin, 1994;
Nate Mason, 1981-83;
Bruce Mathison, 1981-82;
Mark Mauer, 1979-81;
Keithen McCant, 1990-91;
Mike McCashland,
   1982-84;
Maurice McCloney, 1978;
John McCormick,
   1985-87;
Tim McCoy, 1987, '89;
Tim McCrady, 1978-80;
Andre McDuffy, 1991-92;
Mark McElroy, 1981;
Octavious McFarlin,
   1994-96;
John McMillen, 1991-92;
Steve McWhirter,
   1979-82;
Andy Means, 1978-80;
Ken Mehlin, 1991-93;
Jeff Merrell, 1980-82;
Kory Mikos, 1994-96;
Barron Miles, 1992-94;
Paul Miles, 1983-85;
Tom Milius, 1996;
Brian Miller, 1988;
Bryce Miller, 1996;
Cleo Miller, 1985-86;
Dan Miller, 1975;

Junior Miller, 1977-79;
Kevin Miller, 1989;
Todd Millikan, 1985-88;
George Mills, 1973, '75;
Jeff Mills, 1987-89;
Mike Minter, 1993-96;
Johnny Mitchell, 1990-91;
Brian Mohsen, 1990;
Junior Monarrez, 1988-89;
Wonder Monds, 1973-75;
Bruce Moore, 1991-93;
Jeff Moran, 1973-74;
Mark Moravec, 1980-82;
Brett Moritz, 1977;
Tom Morrow, 1983-84;
Kareem Moss, 1992-94;
Brad Muehling, 1982-83;
Abdul Mohammad,
   1991-94;
Brad Mundt, 1991-92;
Marc Munford, 1984-86;
Jim Murphy, 1981-82;
Mike Murray, 1987-89;
Larry Mushinskie,
   1973-75;
Eddie Niel, 1980-81;
Bob Nelson, 1973-74;
Derrie Nelson, 1978-80;
John Nelson, 1987-88;
Ray Nelson, 1985-87;
Keith Nuebert, 1987;
John Nichols, 1986-87;
Jack Noel, 1985;
Danny Noonan, 1984-86;
David Noonan, 1990-93;
John Noonan, 1980;
Sean Noster, 1994;
Brian Nunns, 1994-95;
Chris O'Gara, 1987-89;
Jeff Ogard, 1994-96;
Mike O'Halleran, 1973;
Tom Ohrt, 1976-78;
John O'Leary, 1973-75;
Jeff Olsen, 1993;
Harlan Opie, 1987;
Tony Ortiz, 1996;
Steve Ott, 1992-95;
Mike Otte, 1985;

Woody Paige, 1983-85;
Tony Palmer, 1987;
Rick Panneton, 1974-75;
Stan Parker, 1984-86;
John Parrella, 1990-92;
Kevin Parsons, 1983-86;
Tom Pate, 1973-74;
Dennis Pavelka, 1974;
Jon Pedersen, 1992, '93;
Aaron Penland, 1992-95;
Matt Penland, 1990, '92;
Dan Pensick, 1977-79;
Jeff Perino, 1996;
Jason Pesterfield, 1992-94;
Lawrence Pete, 1986-88;
Christian Peter, 1993-95;
Jason Peter, 1994-96;
Dick Peterson, 1980;
Jerome Peterson, 1996;
Mike Petko, 1989-91;
Lawrence Phillips,
   1993-95;
Ray Phillips, 1975-76;
Brent Pick, 1990;
Bruce Pickens, 1988-90;
Clete Pillen, 1974-76;
Jim Pillen, 1976-78;
Dan Pleasant, 1990-91;
Randy Poeschl, 1976-78;
Brian Pokorny, 1983, '85;
Fred Pollack, 1994-96;
Brett Popplewell, 1992-93;
Scott Porter, 1983-84;
Paul Potadle, 1979;
Ralph Powell, 1973;
Vernon Powell, 1990-91;
Wade Praeuner, 1981-83;
Kelly Prater, 1991;
Jim Prevette, 1993;
Todd Proffott, 1983, '85;
Bryan Pruitt, 1993-94;
Ron Pruitt, 1973-74, '76;
Jeff Pullen, 1975-77;
Tom Punt, 1988-90;
Sean Putnam, 1987-87;
Jeff Quinn, 1978-80;
Kevin Ramaekers,
   1991-93;

Scott Rairdon, 1981-83;
Tom Rathman, 1983-85;
Dave Redding, 1973-75;
Jarvis Redwine, 1979-80;
John Reece, 1989, '91-93;
Gregg Reeves, 1983-85;
Ray Reifenrath, 1990-91;
Brad Reilly, 1990;
John Reinhardt, 1983-84;
Ted Retzlaff, 1995-96;
Rod Reynolds, 1983, '85;
Dan Rice, 1979;
Randy Rick, 1976-77;
Dave Ridder, 1981-83;
Dave Rimington, 1979-82;
Mike Roberts, 1995-96;
Terry Rodgers, 1986,
  '88-89;
John Roschal, 1988-89;
Tim Roth, 1983-85;
Tim Rother, 1986-87;
Guy Rozier, 1983, '85;
Mike Rozier, 1981-83;
Mike Rucker, 1995-96;
Steve Runty, 1973;
John Ruud, 1978-79;
Tom Ruud, 1973-74;
Kelly Saalfeld, 1977-79;
Scott Saltsman, 1994-96;
Tony Samuel, 1975-77;
Marvin Sanders, 1987-89;
Rich Sanger, 1973;
Mark Schellen, 1982-83;
Cory Schlesinger,
  1992-94;
Randy Schleusener,
  1978-80;
Damon Schmadeke, 1993;
Darren Schmadeke,
  1993-95;
Dan Schmidt, 1974-76;
Sam Schmidt, 1987-89;
Bob Schmit, 1973;
Dave Schneider, 1983;
Dean Schneider, 1993;
Gary Schneider, 1982-83,
  '85-86;
Jeff Schneider, 1973;

Craig Schnitzler, 1987;
Robb Schnitzler, 1984-86;
Scott Schoettger, 1982-83;
Brian Schuster, 1994-96;
Jim Scott, 1990-92;
Mike Sculley, 1981;
L.G. Searcey, 1980;
Karem Sears, 1996;
Jim Seeton, 1974;
Kevin Seibel, 1979-82;
David Seizys, 1991-93;
John Selko, 1976;
Jeff Sellentin, 1985-86;
Bill Settles, 1988;
Dave Shamblin, 1973,
  '75-76;
Brian Shaw, 1996;
Matt Shaw, 1992-94;
Pat Shaw, 1986;
Ken Shead, 1983-85;
Von Sheppard, 1985-87;
John Sherlock, 1982-83;
James Sherman, 1996;
Will Shields, 1989-91;
Bryan Seibler, 1984-86;
Tom Seiler, 1991-94;
Jason Simdorn, 1993;
Ricky Simmons, 1980,
  '82-83;
James Sims, 1995-96;
Joe Sims, 1988-90;
Sammy Sims, 1979-81;
Adam Skoda, 1995;
Jim Skow, 1983-85;
Kurt Skadis, 1988;
T.J. Slansky, 1991-92;
Bob Sledge, 1986-88;
Bob Smail, 1981;
Brad Smith, 1983-85;
Jeff Smith, 1982-84;
Kent Smith, 1975-76;
Neil Smith, 1985-87;
Paul Smith, 1981;
Rod Smith, 1985-87;
Tim Smith, 1977-79;
Tom Sorley, 1976-78;
Omar Sots, 1990-91;
Chris Spachman, 1984-86;

Ken Spaeth, 1975-77;
Joe Spitzenberger, 1990;
Todd Spratte, 1981;
Kurt Stacey, 1975;
Brenden Stai, 1991-94;
Steve Stanard, 1987;
Chad Stanley, 1994;
John Starkebaum,
  1973-73;
Anthony Steels, 1979-81;
Dan Steiner, 1978-79;
Dean Steinkuhler,
  1981-83;
Keith Steward, 1976;
Byron Stewart, 1976;
Ed Stewardt, 1991-94;
Mike Stigge, 1989-92;
Eric Stokes, 1993-96;
Scott Strasburger,
  1982-84;
Matt Strasburger, 1985;
John Strasheim, 1987;
Dave Stromath, 1980-81;
Rob Stuckey, 1982-84;
Dean Sukup, 1978-79;
Craig Sundberg, 1982-84;
Dan Svehla, 1988-90;
Shane Swanson, 1982-84;
Chester Talley, 1975;
Aaron Taylor, 1994-96;
Steve Taylor, 1985-88;
Ryan Terwilliger, 1993-96;
Dan Thayer, 1985-86;
Randy Theiss, 1980-82;
Gordon Thiessen, 1978;
Anthony Thomas,
  1982-84;
Bobby Thomas, 1974-76;
Broderick Thomas,
  1985-88;
Tom Thomas, 1975;
Will Thomas, 1989-90;
Jim Thompson, 1982-84;
Bob Thornton, 1973;
Willie Thornton, 1973-74;
Billy Todd, 1977-78;
Travis Toline, 1995-96;
Jared Tomich, 1994-96;

Jeff Tomjack, 1985-87;
Larry Townsend, 1994-95;
Mike Tramner, 1982-83;
Mark Traynowicz,
 1982-84;
Adam Treu, 1994-96;
Scott Tucker, 1983-85;
Matt Turman, 1994-96;
Nate Turner, 1988-91;
Travis Turner, 1984-85;
Pat Tyrance, 1988-90;
Brad Tyrer, 1984-86;
Larry Valasek, 1975-77;
Ray Valladao, 1987-89;
Mike Van Cleave,
 1995-96;
Kris Van Norman,
 1980-82;
Ron VanderMeer, 1976;
Rich Varner, 1975;
Jon Vedral, 1994-96;
Mike Vedral, 1990-92;
Tony Veland, 1992, '94-95;
Tom Vergith, 1980, '82;
Tom Vering, 1977-79;
Steve Volin, 1994-95;
Matt Vrzal, 1994-96;
Doug Waddell, 1991;
Billy Wade, 1992-93;
Brandt Wade, 1995-96;
Henrey Waechter,
 1980-81;
Stan Waldemore, 1975-77;
Cartier Walker, 1987-88;
Kenny Walker, 1989-90;
Eric Walter, 1995-96;
Darrell Walton, 1976-78;
Jim Wanek, 1988-90;
Eric Warfield, 1995-96;
Steve Warren, 1996;
Brain Washington,
 1984-87;
Riley Washington,
 1993-95;
William Washington,
 1989-92;
Dennis Watkins, 1984-85;
Bill Weber, 1981-84;

Kerry Weinmaster,
 1976-79;
Kent Wells, 1987-89;
Doug Welniak, 1985-87;
Tom Welter, 1985-86;
Rick Wendland, 1989-90;
Tom Werner, 1990-92;
Austin Wertz, 1992-93;
Don Westbrook, 1973-74;
Jamie Weyers, 1992;
Jeff Wheeler, 1986;
Daryl White, 1973;
David White, 1989-92;
Freeman White III, 1989;
John White, 1983;
Jerry Wied, 1974-75;
Erik Wiegert, 1989-91;
Zach Wiegert, 1991-94;
Steve Wieser, 1973-74;
Sean Wieting, 1996;
Shevin Wiggins, 1996;
Jim Wightman, 1975-77;
Paul Wightman, 1991;
Dante Wiley, 1986;
Kenn Wilhite, 1991-92;
Doug Wilkening, 1981-82;
Joel Wilks, 1992-94;
Brent Williams, 1978-80;
Daren Williams, 1991-93;
Jamel Williams, 1994-96;
Jamie Williams, 1979-82;
Jimmy Williams, 1979-81;
Toby Williams, 1980-82;
Tyrone Williams, 1993-95;
Aaron Wills, 1996;
Jason Wiltz, 1996;
Dan Wingard, 1983, '85;
Grant Wistrom, 1994-96;
Bob Wolfe, 1973;
Scott Woodard, 1978-81;
Wendell Wooten, 1986,
 '88;
Jamie Worden, 1987-88;
Toby Wright, 1992-93;
Tim Wurth, 1977-79;
Zaven Yaralian, 1973;
Rod Yates, 1983;
Jake Young, 1986-89;

Larry Young, 1976-77;
Dale Zabrocki, 1976;
Andrew Zacharias,
 1989-90;
Tyler Sahn, 1991;
Nick Zanetich, 1974;
Jon Zatechka, 1994-96;
Rob Zatechka, 1991-94;
Bill Ziegelbein, 1990-91;
Mike Zierke, 1983-84;
Chris Zyzda, 1990-92.

**Heisman Trophy Winner Under Osborne**
 Mike Rozier, 1983

**Top 10 Finishers in the Heisman Voting**
 David Humm, 5th, 1974; Jarvis Redwine, 8th, 1980; Dave Rimington, 5th and Mike Rozier, 10th, 1982; Turner Gill, 4th, 1983; Lawrence Phillips, 8th and Zach Wiegert, 9th, 1994; Tommie Frazier, 2nd, 1995.

**National Football Foundation and College Hall of Fame Inductee**
 Dave Rimington, 1979-82

**Osborne's Butkus Award Winner**
 Trev Alberts, 1993

**Other NU Butkus Finalists**
 Broderick Thomas, 2nd, 1988; Ed Stewart, 3rd, 1994

**Osborne's Lombardi Award Winners**
 Dave Rimington, 1982; Dean Steinkuhler, 1983; Grant Wistrom, 1997

**Lombardi Finalists**
 Broderick Thomas, 1988; Zach Wiegert, 1994

**Outland Trophy Winners Under Osborne**
 Dave Rimington, 1981 and 1982; Dean Steinkuhler, 1983; Will Shields, 1992; Zach Wiegert, 1994; Aaron Taylor, 1997.

**Osborne's All-Americans**
 Daryl White, 1973; John Dutton, 1973; Rik Bonness, 1974-75; Marvin Crenshaw, 1974; Dave Humm, 1974; Bob Martin, 1975; Wonder Monds, 1975; Dave Butterfield, 1976; Mike Fultz, 1976; Vince Ferragamo, 1976; Tom Davis, 1977; Kelvin Clark, 1978; George Andrews, 1978; Junior Miller, 1979; Randy Schleusener, 1980; Derrie Nelson, 1980; Jarvis Redwine, 1980; Jimmy Williams, 1981; Dave Rimington, 1981-82; Mike Rozier, 1982-83; Irving Fryar, 1983; Dean Steinkuhler, 1983; Bret Clark, 1984; Harry Grimminger, 1984; Mark Traynowicz, 1984; Bill Lewis, 1985; Jim Skow, 1985; Danny Noonan, 1986; John McCormick, 1987; Neil Smith, 1987; Steve Taylor, 1997; Broderick Thomas, 1987-88; Jake Young, 1988-89; Doug Glaser, 1989; Kenny Walker, 1990; Travis Hill, 1992; Will Shields, 1992; Trev Alberts, 1993; Brenden Stai, 1994; Ed Stewart, 1994; Zach Wiegert, 1994; Tommie Frazier, 1995; Aaron Graham, 1995; Jared Tomich, 1995-96; Grant Wistrom, 1996-97; Aaron Taylor, 1996-97; Jason Peter, 1997.

**Osborne's Academic All-Americans Through 1996**
 Frosty Anderson, 1973; Rik Bonness, 1975; Tom Heiser, 1975; Vince Ferragamo, 1976; Ted Harvey, 1976-77; Jim Pillen, 1978; George Andrews, 1978; Rod Horn, 1979;

Randy Schleusener, 1979-80; Kelly Saalfeld, 1979; Jeff Finn, 1980; Ric Lindquist, 1981; Randy Theiss, 1981; Dave Rimington, 1981-82; Scott Strasburger, 1983-84; Rob Stuckey, 1983-84; Mark Traynowicz, 1984; Dale Klein, 1986; Tom Welter, 1986; Jeff Jamrog, 1987; Mark Blazek, 1987-88; John Koreker, 1988; Gerry Gdowski, 1989; Jake Young, 1989; David Edeal, 1990; Pat Tyrance, 1990; Jim Wanek, 1990; Pat Englebart, 1991; Mike Stigge, 1991-92; Trev Alberts, 1993; Terry Connealy, 1993-94; Rob Zatechka, 1993-94; Matt Shaw, 1994; Aaron Graham, 1995; Grant Wistrom, 1996.

**Top 8 Award Winners**

Randy Schleusener and Dave Rimington, 1981; Mark Traynowicz, 1985; Jake Young, 1990; Pat Tyrance, 1991; Trev Alberts, 1993; Aaron Graham, 1995; Grant Wistrom, 1997.